P9-CAA-298

BY COLUM McCANN

FICTION

Thirteen Ways of Looking

TransAtlantic

Let the Great World Spin

Zoli

Dancer

Everything in This Country Must

This Side of Brightness

Songdogs

Fishing the Sloe-Back River

NONFICTION

Letters to a Young Writer

The Book of Men (editor)

LETTERS TO A
YOUNG WRITER

LETTERS TO A
YOUNG WRITER

Some Practical

and

Philosophical

Advice

COLUM McCANN

RANDOM HOUSE

NEW YORK

Copyright © 2017 by Colum McCann

All rights reserved.

Published in the United States by Random House,
an imprint and division of Penguin Random House LLC,
New York.

RANDOM HOUSE and the HOUSE colophon
are registered trademarks of Penguin
Random House LLC.

Hardback ISBN 978-0-399-59080-1
Ebook ISBN 978-0-399-59081-8

Printed in the United States of America on
acid-free paper

randomhousebooks.com

987654321

First Edition

Title-page photograph by Kalin Ivanov

Book design by Barbara M. Bachman

For Jennifer Raab,

Sarah Chalfant,

Alexandra Pringle, and

Jennifer Hershey.

And for all the young

writers you have

brought to the world.

CONTENTS

CONTENTS

CONTENTS

The Unsayable Ecstasies

"NOBODY CAN ADVISE YOU AND HELP you, nobody," said Rilke in *Letters to a Young Poet* over a century ago. "There is only one way. Go into yourself."

Rilke, of course, was right—nobody but yourself can help. In the end it all comes down to the strike of the word upon the page, not to mention the strike thereafter, and the strike after that. But Rilke was taken by the request from the young writer, and he corresponded with Franz Xaver Kappus in ten letters over the course of six years. Rilke's was advice on matters of religion, love, feminism, sex, art, solitude, and patience, but it was also keyed in to the life of the poet and how these things might shape the words upon the page.

"This most of all," he says. "Ask yourself in the most silent hour of night: Must I write?"

Everybody who has ever felt the need to write knows the silent hour. I have come upon many such people—and indeed many such hours— during my writing and teaching life. Each year my first class in the Hunter College MFA program begins with the statement that I won't be able to teach the students anything at all. This comes as a bit of a shock to the twelve young men and women who have decided to devote themselves to the crafty, sullen art. These are among the smartest young writers in America, six first years, six second years, who have been chosen from a pool of many hundreds. I don't mean my opening statement to them every semester as an act of discouragement: it is, I hope, the exact opposite. *I can teach you nothing. Now that you know this, go learn.* In the end I'm guiding them toward the fire in the hope that they will recognize the places where they will, most certainly, be burned. But the advice is also given in the hope that they learn how to handle, and pass along, the fire.

One of the best places for young writers to be is facing the burning wall, with only the virtues of stamina, desire, and perseverance to propel them across to the other side. And breach the wall they do: some tunnel, some climb, some bulldoze. Not with my help, but by going properly inside themselves, *à la Rilke*. I've been teaching now for the best part of twenty years. That's a lot of chalk and a lot of red pencil. I haven't loved every minute of it, but I've loved most, and I wouldn't swap the experience for the world. There's been a National Book Award for one student. A Booker Prize for another. Guggenheims. Pushcarts. Mentorships. Friendships. But let's be honest, there has been burnout too. There's been weeping and gnashing of teeth. There have been walkouts. Collapses. Regret.

The fact of the matter is that I'm only there as a foil. Practice and time do not necessarily bestow seniority. A student might—at the very beginning—

know so much more than I know. Still, the only hope is that I might say one or two things over the course of a couple of semesters that might save them a little time and heartbreak.

All of those students, bar none, are looking, in Rilke's words, "to say ecstasies that are unsayable." The unsayable indeed. The job is theirs. The ability to trust in the difficult. The tenacity to understand that it takes time and patience to succeed.

Not so long ago I was asked by StoryPrize.org to write a short piece about the writing life. I mashed together some of my ideas, mixed it with a little credo and whatever wisdom I might be able to wring out of the dishtowel of teaching days. I called it "Letter to a Young Writer," and it is the first entry in this book. Other entries followed over the course of a year. They were there, at times, for instruction. At other times they were clarion calls. This, then, is not a Writer's Manual. Nor is it, I hope, a rant. It's more a whisper while out walking in the park, something else I like to do with my students at times. I imagined it as a word in the ear of a young writer, though it could, I suppose, be a series of letters to any writer, not least myself.

I'm reminded, of course, of Cyril Connolly's line: "How many books did Renoir write on how to paint?" I understand that it could be folly to try to dissect what is essentially a mysterious process, but in spite of that, here it is, with the full knowledge that opening up the magic box might doom its readers to disappointment. Still, the truth is that I genuinely enjoy watching young writers begin to put a shape on the contents of their world. I push my students hard. Sometimes they push back. In fact one of my opening workshop tenets is that blood will inevitably seep out the door during the course of a semester, and invariably some of that blood is my own.

In putting together these words, I have, I admit, failed miserably—which is, as you will see, a bit of a back-slap for myself. I covet failure. I have done it here. This advice comes up short of any I would want to receive myself. I deliver it, I hope, with a humble bow and a desire to get out of its way.

A word of warning. Once, when writing a novel called *Dancer,* a fictionalization of the life of Rudolf Nureyev, I sent the manuscript to a hero of mine. This was a writer whose every word I absolutely coveted. He was inordinately kind and sent me back six handwritten pages of notes. I took virtually every single suggestion, but I was disturbed about one. He said that I should cut the opening war soliloquy that begins "Four winters . . ." I had spent close to six months on this section and it was among my favorite parts of the book. He made a good argument against keeping it, but I was still upset. For days on end I walked around with his voice in my head. *Cut it, cut it, cut it.* How could I go against the advice of one of the world's greatest writers?

In the end I didn't take his counsel. I stepped inside and listened to myself. When the book finally came out, he wrote to tell me that I had made the correct choice and he had been humbly wrong. It is one of the most beautiful letters I have ever received. John Berger. I name him because he was my teacher, not in a literal sense but in a textural way and in the manner of a friend. I have had several other teachers too: Jim Kells; Pat O'Connell; Brother Gerard Kelly; my father, Sean McCann; Benedict Kiely; Jim Harrison; Frank McCourt; Edna O'Brien; Peter Carey; along with virtually every writer I have ever read. I am indebted also to Dana Czapnik, Cindy Wu, Ellis Maxwell, and my son John Michael for help with this book. The voice we get is not just one voice. We receive ours from a series of elsewheres. This is the spark.

I hope there is something here for any young writer—or any older writer, for that matter—who happens to be looking for a teacher to come along, a teacher who, in the end, can really teach nothing at all but fire.

LETTERS TO A

YOUNG WRITER

LETTER TO A
YOUNG WRITER

*I live my life in widening circles that reach
out across the world.*

—RAINER MARIA RILKE

DO THE THINGS THAT DO NOT COMPUTE.
Be earnest. Be devoted. Be subversive of ease. Read
aloud. Risk yourself. Do not be afraid of sentiment
even when others call it sentimentality. Be ready to
get ripped to pieces: it happens. Permit yourself
anger. Fail. Take pause. Accept the rejections. Be
vivified by collapse. Practice resuscitation. Have
wonder. Bear your portion of the world. Find a
reader you trust. They must trust you back. Be a
student, not a teacher, even when you teach. Don't
B.S. yourself. If you believe the good reviews, you

must believe the bad. Still, don't hammer yourself down. Do not allow your heart to harden. Face it, the cynics have better one-liners than we do. Take heart: they can never finish their stories. Enjoy difficulty. Embrace mystery. Find the universal in the local. Put your faith in language—character will follow and plot, too, will eventually emerge. Push yourself further. Do not tread water. It is possible to survive that way, but impossible to write. Never be satisfied. Transcend the personal. Have trust in the staying power of what is good. We get our voice from the voices of others. Read promiscuously. Imitate, copy, but become your own voice. Write about that which you want to know. Better still, write toward that which you don't know. The best work comes from outside yourself. Only then will it reach within. Be bold in the face of the blank sheet. Restore what has been ridiculed by others. Write beyond despair. Make justice from reality. Sing. Make vision from the dark. The considered grief is so much better than the unconsidered. Be suspicious of that which gives you too much consolation. Hope and belief and faith will fail you often, but so what? Share your rage. Resist. Denounce. Have stamina. Have courage. Have perseverance. The quiet lines matter as much as the noisy ones. Trust your blue pencil, but don't forget the red one. Make the essential count. Allow your fear. Give yourself permission. You have something to write about. Just because it's narrow doesn't mean it's not universal. Don't be didactic—nothing kills life quite so much as explanation. Make an argument for the imagined. Begin with doubt. Be an explorer, not a tourist. Go somewhere nobody else has gone. Fight for repair. Believe in detail. Unique your language. A story begins long before its first word. It ends long after its last. Make the ordinary sublime. Don't panic. Reveal a truth that isn't yet there. At the same time, entertain. Satisfy the appetite for seriousness and joy. Dilate your nostrils. Fill your lungs with language. A lot can be taken from you—even your life—but not your stories about that life. So this, then, is a word, not without love and respect, to a young writer: write.

THERE ARE NO RULES

There are three rules for writing a novel.
Unfortunately, no one knows what they are.
—W. SOMERSET MAUGHAM

HERE ARE NO RULES. OR IF THERE ARE any rules, they are only there to be broken. Embrace these contradictions. You must be prepared to hold two or more opposing ideas in the palms of your hands at the exact same time.

To hell with grammar, but only if you know the grammar first. To hell with formality, but only if you have learned what it means to be formal. To hell with plot, but you better at some stage make something happen. To hell with structure, but only if you have thought it through so thoroughly that

you can safely walk through your work with your
eyes closed.

The great ones break the rules on purpose. They
do it in order to remake the language. They say it
like nobody has ever said it before. And then they
unsay it, and they keep unsaying it, breaking their
own rules over and over again.

So be adventurous in breaking—or maybe even
making—the rules.

YOUR FIRST LINE

> *The first sentence of every novel should be:*
> *"Trust me, this will take time but there is*
> *order here, very faint, very human."*
>
> —MICHAEL ONDAATJE

A FIRST LINE SHOULD OPEN UP YOUR rib cage. It should reach in and twist your heart backward. It should suggest that the world will never be the same again.

The opening salvo should be active. It should plunge your reader into something urgent, interesting, informative. It should move your story, your poem, your play, forward. It should whisper in your reader's ear that everything is about to change.

So much of what then follows is based on the tone of the opening cue. Assure us that the world is not static. Give us something concrete to hang on to. Let us know that we're going somewhere. But take it easy too. Don't stuff the world into your first page. Achieve a balance. Let the story unfold. Think of it as a doorway. Once you get your readers over the threshold, you can show them around the rest of the house. At the same time, don't panic if you don't get it right first time around. Often the opening line won't be found until you're halfway through your first draft. You hit page 157 and you suddenly realize, *Ah, that's where I should have begun.*

So you go back and begin again.

Open elegantly. Open fiercely. Open delicately. Open with surprise. Open with everything at stake. This, of course, is a bit like being told to walk a tightrope. Go ahead, then, walk the tightrope! Relax yourself into the tension of the wire. The first line, like the first step, is only the first of many, yet it sets the shape of what is to come. Try walking a foot off the ground, then two feet, then three. Eventually you might go a quarter mile in the sky.

Then again, you might stumble and fall. No matter. It is, after all, a work of the imagination. You won't die trying.

At least not yet.

DON'T WRITE WHAT YOU KNOW

The inexecutable is all I'm interested in.

—NATHAN ENGLANDER

DON'T WRITE WHAT YOU KNOW, WRITE toward what you *want to know*.

Step out of your skin. Risk yourself. This opens up the world. Go to another place. Investigate what lies beyond your curtains, beyond the wall, beyond the corner, beyond your town, beyond the edges of your own known country.

A writer is an explorer. She knows she wants to get somewhere, but she doesn't know if the somewhere even exists yet. It is still to be created. A Galápagos of the imagination. A whole new theory of who we are.

Don't sit around looking inward. That's boring. In the end your navel contains only lint. You have to propel yourself outward, young writer. Think about others, think about elsewhere, think about a distance that will bring you, eventually, back home.

The only true way to expand your world is to inhabit an otherness beyond ourselves. There is one simple word for this: *empathy*. Don't let them fool you. Empathy is violent. Empathy is tough. Empathy can rip you open. Once you go there, you can be changed. Get ready: they will label you sentimental. But the truth is that the cynics are the sentimental ones. They live in a cloud of their own limited nostalgia. They have no muscularity at all. They remain in one place. They have one idea and it sparks nothing else. Remember, the world is so much more than one story. We find in others the ongoing of ourselves.

So, leave the cynics be. Out-cynic them. Step into that elsewhere. Believe that your story is bigger than yourself.

In the end, of course, your first-grade teacher

was correct: we can, indeed, only write what we know. It is logically and philosophically impossible to do otherwise. But if we write *toward* what we don't supposedly know, we will find out what we knew but weren't yet entirely aware of. We will have made a shotgun leap in our consciousness. We will not be stuck in the permanent backspin of *me, me, me.*

As Vonnegut says, we should be continually jumping off cliffs and developing our wings on the way down.

THE TERROR OF THE
WHITE PAGE

The pleasure of abiding. The pleasure of insistence, of persistence. The pleasure of obligation, the pleasure of dependency. The pleasures of ordinary devotion.

—MAGGIE NELSON

DON'T LET THE TERROR OF THE WHITE page shrink-wrap your mind. The excuse that you have writer's block is far too easy. You have to show up for work. You have to sit in the chair and fight the blankness. Don't leave your desk. Don't abandon the room. Don't go off to pay the bills. Don't wash the dishes. Don't check the sports pages. Don't open the mail. Don't distract yourself in any way until you feel you have fought and tried.

You have to put in the time. If you are not there, the words will not appear. Simple as that.

A writer is not someone who thinks obsessively about writing, or talks about it, or plans it, or dissects it, or even reveres it: a writer is the one who puts his arse in the chair when the last thing he wants to do is have his arse in the chair.

Good writing will knock the living daylights out of you. Very few people talk about it, but writers have to have the stamina of world-class athletes. The exhaustion of sitting in the one place. The errors. The retrieval. The mental taxation. The dropping of the bucket down into the near-empty well over and over again. Moving a word around a page. Moving it back again. Questioning it. Doubting it. Trying it in **bold.** Looking at it in *italic.* Increasing the font size. Spelling it differently. Putting it in another accent. Shifting it around again and again. Single space, double space, justify right and left, go back to single space. Sounding it out. Figuring the best way to leave it alone. Hanging in there as the clock ticks on. Not conceding victory to the negative. Railing against the attractively defeatist. Understanding not only what words are for, but also what words stand against. Getting up off the ground when you've punched yourself to the floor. Dusting yourself off. Readjusting your mouth guard. Sustaining what you have inherited from previous days of work.

Don't worry so much about your word count. Your word *cut* is more important. You have to sit there sharpening that red pencil or hitting the delete button or flinging the pages into the fire. Often, the more words you cut, the better. A good day might actually be a hundred words *less* than you had yesterday. Even no words on the page is better than no time at the page at all.

Insist on your own persistence. The words will come. They might not arrive as burning bushes or pillars of light, but no matter. Fight again, then again and again. If you fight long enough, the right word will arrive, and if it doesn't, at least you tried.

Just keep your arse in the chair. Arse in the chair. Arse in the chair.

Stare the blank page down.

NO IDEAS WITHOUT MUSIC

> *The relation between what we see and what*
> *we know is never settled. Each evening we*
> *see the sun set. We know that the earth is*
> *turning away from it. Yet the knowledge, the*
> *explanation, never quite fits the sight.*
>
> —JOHN BERGER

IT'S RIDICULED AS THE MOST INANE
question, but still everyone asks it: Where do they
come from, these ideas of yours? Guess what?
Much of the time a writer doesn't actually know.
They're just there. They have arrived unbidden. You
hit on something that grabs the muscle of your
imagination and begins to tighten down upon
you until you feel a cramp. This cramp is called

obsession. This is what writers do: we write toward our obsessions. You will not be able to let it go until you find words to confront it. It is the only way that you will free yourself.

The trick is that you have to be open to the world. You have to be listening. And you have to be watching. You have to be alive to inspiration. The general idea may come from the newspaper, it may come from a line overheard on the subway, it may be the story that was sitting in the family attic. It could have come from a photograph, or another book, or it might have sideswiped you for no good reason that you can yet discern. It might even be the general desire to confront a larger issue—the rape of the environment, the root causes of jetliners flown into buildings, the endlessly awful election newsreels unfolding in front of our eyes. No matter. No one story towers over any other. All you know is that it has to be made new to the world and you must begin to investigate it.

Careful, though. Ideas on their own may be fine, and they may make good politics, but they will not necessarily make good literature. You must find the human music first. The thing that outstrips the general idea. The quark of the theory. The grace note within.

You begin with a small detail and you work outward toward your obsession. You are not here to represent cultures or grand philosophies. You don't speak *for* people, but *with* people. You are here to rip open the accepted world and create it new. Often a writer will not know the true reason for writing until long after the work is finished. It is when she gives it to others that its purpose becomes apparent.

To not know exactly where your story is going is a good thing. It may drive you mad for a little while, but there's worse things than madness: try silence, for instance.

A HERO OF
CONSCIOUSNESS

Because this business of becoming conscious, of being a writer, is ultimately about asking yourself, How alive am I willing to be?

—ANNE LAMOTT

THE WHOLE POINT OF GOOD LITERATURE is to make newness durable. You are creating alternative time. You are making vivid that which did not exist before. You are not just the clockmaker, but the measure of the clockmaker's creation. You are shaping past, present, and future. This is quite a responsibility. Respect it.

Guide your reader into the story. Trust me, you say, this may be a long trip, a strange one, a difficult one, a painful one, but eventually it will be worthwhile. At the right moment you can create miracles.

Finding the "moment" of the story—or even the "moment" of a scene—can be one of the great revelations of the writing process. You recognize what this moment means: it is the point at which everything changes, not only for your characters but for you as well. You are getting to the heart of what matters. The fulcrum. The crux. If you miss it, everything else will fall apart.

Your duty is to make the reader see and hear. With the right word, you will find the balance of imaginative richness and form. You have to drag the moment reluctantly from silence. As a writer, you are alive to every sentence. Your imagination is creating a reality. It is as if you are unpeeling time. You gain new territory. You become a hero of consciousness.

All well and good, young writer—*a hero of consciousness* indeed—but be aware that this will cost you effort and pain. You will tear your hair out. Grind your teeth. Rinse your heart out again and again. You will think yourself in constant rehearsal for a performance that might never arrive.

One day you might find yourself hating writing precisely because you want to make it so good. Yet this awful truth is just another form of joy. Get used to it. The sun also sets in order to rise.

OUT FROM THE DUST: CREATING CHARACTERS

Then the writing became so fluid that I sometimes felt as if I were writing for the sheer pleasure of telling a story, which may be the human condition that most resembles levitation.

—GABRIEL GARCÍA MÁRQUEZ

ONE OF THE GREAT JOYS OF FICTION writing is discovering who your character truly is. There is little better than creating someone from the dust of your imagination. But inventing a character from scratch is not simply a matter of ransacking the low shelves of the nearest fiction-supermarket. Your characters must be intricate, complicated, flawed. They need to step up and bear the weight of reality. They need to be a heartbreaking mess of flesh and bone.

We tend to think and analyze in broad sweeping characteristics (honesty, perception, integrity, etc.), but for the purposes of good storytelling you must know your character in the most exact detail. Forget all the chatter about protagonist and antagonist, and all the workshop riffs about dynamic characters or static characters—what you must do is create someone *real*. A common saying in literature is that "character determines fate," which (probably) means that a well-drawn character will take actions consistent with his/her motivations. So, character helps determine a specific outcome in the story. But the story will be nothing if the character is not part of a great human stew. We have to make them so utterly real that the reader can never forget them.

Writing a character into being is like meeting someone you want to fall in love with. You don't care (yet) about the facts of his/her life. Don't overload us with too much information. Allow that to seep out later. We are attracted by a moment in time—a singular moment of flux or change or collapse—not by grand résumés or curricula vitae. So don't generalize. Be specific. Go granular. The reader must fall in love with your characters quickly (or indeed, learn to hate them quickly). We have to have something happen to them: something that jolts our tired hearts awake. Make it traumatic, make it mournful, make it jubilant, it doesn't matter—just allow your reader to care for the physical body that your words evoke, the person behind the language. Later on in the story we can settle down with them and get to know them in a wider sense.

Sometimes we take a character from our own immediate lives and we build a new person upon that scarecrow. Or sometimes we take well-known characters in history and shape them in new ways. Either way we have a responsibility to write them into life. You owe as much to your imagination as you do to history.

They may be made up, but your fictional characters will eventually become real in the world. Jay Gatsby is real. Tom Joad is real. Leopold Bloom is real. (Or at least as real as the seven billion people in the world that we haven't yet met.)

In the end you should probably know your characters as well as you know yourself. Not only what they had for breakfast this morning, but what they *wanted* to have for breakfast. This little slice of literary bacon won't necessarily appear in your story, but you must know it all the same. In fact, the answer to just about any question at all should be on the tip of your tongue. Where was your character born? What is her first memory? What does her handwriting look like? How does she cross at traffic lights? Why is there a burn mark at the base of her forefinger? Why is it that she limps? Why is there dirt under the fingernails? Where did the hip scar come from? Who would she vote for? What is the first item she shoplifted? What makes her happy? What terrifies her? What does she feel most guilty about? (You'd be amazed how many writers never even ask these simple things of their characters.)

You should be able to close your eyes and dwell inside that character's body. The sound of her voice. The texture of her footsteps. Walk around with her for a while. Let her dwell in the rattlebag of your head. Make a mental list of who/what she is, where she comes from. Appearance. Body language. Unique mannerisms. Childhood. Conflicts. Desires. Voice. Allow your characters to surprise you. When it seems they should go right, send them left. When they appear too joyful, break them. When they want to leave the page, force them to stay a sentence longer. Complicate them. Conflict them. Give them forked tongues. This is what real life is all about. Don't be too logical. Logic can paralyze us.

In the end, if you don't know your character, sit down and write a letter to her. Your first line might be: *Why don't I know you?* You might be surprised by the reply. It is, after all, you writing back to yourself.

Does this sound extreme? So be it. It's extreme. Writing goes to all the extremities.

Nabokov says that his characters are just his galley slaves—but he's Nabokov, and he's allowed to say things like that. Let me respectfully disagree. Your characters deserve your respect. Some reverence. Some life of their own. You must thank them for surprising you, and for ringing the doorbell of your imagination.

Tell the truth through whichever veil comes to hand—but tell it. Resign yourself to the lifelong sadness that comes from never being satisfied.

—ZADIE SMITH

GOOD WRITING IS ART AND VERISI-militude both. This applies to fiction, nonfiction, plays, and poems, even journalism. We have to hold the possibilities of truth and invention together in the exact same place. The truth must be shaped. And it needs a lot of work in order to get there.

Some people seem to think that invention is about telling lies. Far from it. Invention is about carving out the authentic. We use our imaginations in order to access the deepest darkdown things.

In the end it is only the well-chosen word, whether ornate or bare, that is capable of dealing with truth. This word, or this series of words, must give shape to the brutality of our lives, but it also must give meaning and credence to the destruction of that brutality. Only that language which is capable of reaching the poetic will be able to stand in opposition to that which is wrong. In other words, nothing short of your best work will do. Language is a great weapon. It must be complicated, layered, even frustrating. It must be felt. It can be astounding, or confounding. It should say the things we knew, but hadn't yet made sense of. It should give us pause. It should make us nod. It should give us silence. This is not about lying, it is about shaping, molding, guiding. It has to be true to your spirit of invention.

And what is this supposed "truth" anyway? Maybe truth is that which the world is aware of, but does not yet know. It is your job as a writer to tell the world something it does not already know. This is easily said, but difficult, maybe impossible, to do.

Still, seek out those truths that are not self-evident. The more freedom a writer has, the more she must become a critic of the place she lives. Look around you. Depth begins at home. Find out what is wrong and then begin to write about it, in order to write *away* from it. Even if you're creating an *elsewhere,* you are still writing about what is close to home. You don't owe allegiance to your government. Nor to accepted ideas. But you do owe allegiance to that elusive notion of truth. Elusive, why? Because once you have found it, it has probably already changed into something new, something even more pernicious. There will always be new cruelties to confront. New problems to occupy. In the end writing solves nothing. Be joyful about that. But—at the same time—never forget that it matters. Do I contradict myself? Very well then, I contradict myself. Whitman says we contain multitudes. Joyce says that good writing re-creates life out of life. Who are we to argue with the greats? Just strike the word down on the page. No preaching involved. No sermonizing. No pointless barking at the passing streams. Just earnest endeavor and grit. A true mining of your world. The ability to force yourself into the darkest corner in order to discover something that hasn't yet been said.

Yes, I know, these words are so easily conjured up, and so difficult to accomplish, but no matter, you have to do it. Look closely at yourself, your community, your loved ones. Speak out. You should write so as not to fall silent. That's the truth, or the closest we might get.

In the end we are bound to court and even favor disappointment. We finally understand that there is no absolute truth at all. Still, what should continually interest you is the difference between authentic thought and flotsam, between honesty and intellectual flummery. So, just because something actually happened to you does not mean that it will make a true story, or even a good story. Just because someone said it in "real" life doesn't make it superior. Just because someone says it is true doesn't mean that it's actually true. Make it true. Imagine it into reality. Take the real world and put layers on it. Just keep it honest. And your best work will emerge. Truly.

CARRY A NOTEBOOK

*The role of a writer is not to say what we can
all say, but what we are unable to say.*

—ANAÏS NIN

Carry a notebook. Find one small
and pliable enough to fit in your pocket, slim
enough that it doesn't weigh you down. Be judi-
cious with it. Don't spend your day with your face
in its pages, but write in it when you get a chance.
Images, ideas, snatches of street dialogue, addresses,
descriptions, whatever might eventually make its
way into a sentence. The smallest detail might be
key to a whole new way of thinking. These are
small sparks that might eventually illuminate a
whole book with their light. Fill it up. Date the

notes if you can. Don't lose it. Please don't lose it. Write your address and phone number in the inside flap. Ask anyone who finds it to please return it: offer a small reward. But if you do lose it, don't despair—a good image should have tattooed itself on your brain anyway.

BE A CAMERA

> *This is the essential, aesthetic factor—rhythm,*
> *the harmonious rhythm of relationships. And*
> *when a fortunate rhythm has been struck by*
> *the artist, you experience a radiance. You are*
> *held in aesthetic arrest. That is the epiphany.*
>
> —JOSEPH CAMPBELL

BE A CAMERA. "LANGUAGE" US INTO vision. Make us feel as if we are there. Colors, sounds, sights. Bring us to the pulse of the moment. See the whole landscape at first, then focus in on a detail, and bring that detail to life.

It is a good trick to assume that you have a number of changeable lenses. Be fish-eye. Be wide-angle. Be telephoto. Zoom in. Zoom out. Distort.

Sharpen. Divide. Imagine yourself into the actual camera. Find the words that are glass and shutter both. This is your mind's eye.

A writer is capable of all sorts of agility: even if you force yourself into a narrative rigidity, you can still go just about anywhere. The mind is acrobatic. There is no harm in trying all angles. Try first person, second person, third person. Try from the viewpoint of your main character, then try it from the perspective of the outsider. Sometimes the outsider is the one who makes absolute sense. Shake it up. Faulkner it. DeLillo it. Go from present to past. Attempt the future.

This camerawork relates to a form of presentation too. Be mindful of how the words appear on the page. Line breaks can be vital. Paragraphs. Spaces. Dashes. Ellipses. Keep looking at the words, testing them, probing them. From every angle. Kaleidoscopically.

Eventually—if you persevere as the camera and operator both—you will hear the right voice, and you will see the right form, and you will uncover the right structure, and it will unfold from there. Then you will learn that you are not just a series of moveable parts. You are light-years beyond a machine. You are inside the issues of the human heart. The camera is gone and you have begun to really see.

FUHGEDDABOUDIT: WRITING DIALOGUE

The declared meaning of a spoken sentence is only its overcoat, and the real meaning lies underneath its scarves and buttons.

—PETER CAREY

FUHGEDDABOUDIT. DIALOGUE ON THE PAGE is never real. You could go out this moment and tape a story being told on the street and then transcribe it, but even then it will probably never seem absolutely true.

A dialogue might not be true, but it must be honest. And what it must do is have the *appearance* of ease. It must look as if it just naturally slipped its way onto the page. A properly written piece of dialogue will complement all your surrounding sentences.

There are so many rules, or suggestions, when it comes to dialogue. Forget the *ummm* and forget the *errr*s: they don't translate on the page. Try not to use dialogue to convey information, or at least a slab of obvious information. Interruptions are great. Try writing a conversation between three, four, five people. Let the dialogue work for itself. Use *he said* and *she said,* but avoid clumsy descriptions. Forget about the overblown gasping, exclaiming, insisting, bellowing.

Make your dialogue distinct from the surrounding description, not just in rhythm but in length too. It will break up the prose. Have it be a respite on the page, or have it tee up the words that are about to come. Increase the stumbles and the restarts: a character repeating himself on the page is not necessarily a bad thing.

Make each character distinct. Give them verbal tics. And never forget that people talk away from what they really mean. Lies are very interesting when they emerge in speech. Make action occur within the conversation. Seldom begin in the beginning: catch the dialogue halfway through. No need for *hello*s or *howareyou*s. No need for *goodbye*s either. Jump out from the conversation long before it truly finishes.

Remember that mystery is the glue that joins us: we love the unheard. The reader becomes the most complicit eavesdropper.

Even if using dialect, or patois, or Dublinese, you must realize that there is a reader at the end of the sentence. Don't confuse them. Don't knock them out of the story. A wee bit is enough to get a Northern Irish accent. Don't go Oirish on yourself. Don't fall into stereotype. No *arragh bejaysus* and *begob*. No overdone Southern twang. It'll make y'all wanna holler. No Jamaican overdose, mahn. No Bhrrooklyn nasal noise.

Rather, suggest the music in the reader's brain in the most subtle way. That's enough. One little clue is all you need to give. The reader will take it from there. The dialogue will dialogue itself. Follow it. Don't get too caught up in mirroring reality.

And, hallelujah, written dialogue doesn't have to

follow grammatical rules. Mess up your sentences as much as you want. You have freedom to roam. Freedom to explore. What boundaries can you cross? To signal dialogue, do you use quotation marks? Do you use dashes? Do you use italics? The truth is that you can use all three, even within the same novel and perhaps even within the same story. It's a way of giving an accent to your words.

In shorthand terms, quotation marks are the norm, the dashes are experimental, the italics can be torturously poetic. Using no indicator of dialogue at all is a real bravery on a writer's part, but it can be very effective when done properly.

Study the masters. Roddy Doyle. Louise Erdrich. Elmore Leonard. Marlon James. And always remember that what we don't say is as important as, if not more so than, what we do. So study the silences too, and have them working on the page. You soon find out how loud the silence really is. Everything unsaid leads eventually to what is said.

READ ALOUD

To me, the greatest pleasure of writing is not what it's about, but the music the words make.

—TRUMAN CAPOTE

HAVE A CONVERSATION WITH WHAT you write. Read your work aloud. Walk around your house and forge your way through the ceiling. The sky is more interesting than ceilings anyway. So don't just whisper it: speak it ALOUD. Risk the embarrassment. Take the slagging. Put some throat in your work.

Your partner, your roommate, your friend, your child, may think you're mad, but that is perfectly all right—sanity is overrated anyway.

You need to hear the rhythm of your words. The repetitions. The assonance. The alliteration. The onomatopoeia. The music of it all. Be John Coltrane. Toni Morrison. Gerard Manley Hopkins. Find the inscape of your language. Create new words. Find the infinite jazz. Discover the dappled dawnness.

When you read aloud, you hear the original intent. You see where the music works and where it falls away. You discover rhythm, or the lack of it. You uncover rhymes. And you also find many mistakes. Be happy to discover them. Take your red pencil to them. Cross them out. Find a new word, or a series of words. Then read aloud again and again until it's working. Become the actor you always wanted to be. Find the music: rap or funk or fox-trot, it doesn't matter. Tape yourself with a recorder if you have to. Listen again. Let your sentences form a landscape. The idea of *joy* might need a long crazy ungrammatical sentence running on foolishly yeah breathlessly without care or custom just rapture pureness moving as if there's a horse galloping underneath the words. *Sadness,* on the other hand, might need to be curt. Sharp. Dark. Alone.

Reading aloud will also bring you to new places. You are suddenly out of your house. You're going somewhere new. Don't be afraid of getting lost. Journey as far as you can. Find the dusk and the gloom. Fill your lungs with it. It's the only way you'll negotiate the light. Be worried. That's okay. The dark is something to sound out too.

Brecht asked if there would be singing in the dark times, and he answered that yes, there would be singing *about* the dark times.

They are indeed dark times: be thankful. Sing them.

WHO WHAT WHERE WHEN HOW AND WHY

> *The aim of every artist is to arrest motion,*
> *which is life, by artificial means and hold it*
> *fixed so that a hundred years later, when a*
> *stranger looks at it, it moves again since it*
> *is life.*
>
> —WILLIAM FAULKNER

T HE SIMPLEST QUESTIONS ARE SOME-
times the hardest, but the who-what-where-when-
how-why construction is the fuel of the writer's
fire.

If you have an omniscient or third-person narrator, that's fair enough, you're God, and God gets
away with just about everything (even Her own
capitalization). But if you're doing a first-person

narration, you have to ask yourself a lot of very important questions.

Who is telling the story? This is possibly the easiest one, though it may take a while to determine their exact nature. You decide on a narrator and you begin to breathe life into them: embark on that adventure. It may even be told by multiple first-person narrators, but you should know them inside out.

What happens? This is commonly called plot (more on that conundrum later), but it is also helixed in with all the other questions. What happens is influenced by the who and the where and the why. The narrator will only tell his version of events. He or she may or may not be unreliable (in fact, nearly every first-person narrator is essentially unreliable). The *what* is the human music of time ticking.

Where are they telling it from? This is a tougher proposition. You must imagine the geography of the place from which your character has decided to tell the story. Imagine the very room, the city, the countryside, the ship, in which they dwell. This is the place in which they have chosen to narrate the story and it is key to how the story gets told. Even the wallpaper affects the nature of our words. The table. The window. The hospital bed. The jail cell. The laptop. The tape recorder.

Never forget this—place affects language. It always has and always will. Telling a story from the Birmingham jail is a lot different than telling the story from the banks of the Mississippi. Telling a story from 7 Eccles Street is a lot different than telling the story from a bordello in Zurich. So, consider carefully where your narrator is sitting when they tell their story.

When in time are they telling the story? This one's crucial and something even the best writers often tend to forget. From what point in time is something remembered? Telling a story that happened yesterday is a lot different from telling a story that happened ten or twenty years ago. The moment of the drama is inherently changed. Time has shifted us. You must know at what point they

have decided to open their veins to the story.
Make a decision and stick to it. Time is distance.
Distance is perspective. Perspective is all about
language. So, know all three to enable the fourth.
And then let the story unfold in whatever time
seems true. (The present tense of a first-person
narration is very tricky indeed—how can someone
be telling a story while they are simultaneously
experiencing it?) You must discover the moment of
the story. This is the thing upon which everything
hinges. When is the absolute moment? When did
the world change? When did the clock hands stop?

How does it tie in with everything that has
gone before? How has it unspooled itself into the
world? How have things happened? How is it that
we have learned to remember, or catch the moment
in flight?

And finally—and this one may be the most elusive—do you know **why** your narrator is telling the
story? Everyone tells their story for a reason. To
heal, to murder, to steal, to re-create. To fall in love,
to fall out of love. To annihilate. To titillate. And

even when she tells the story just to make us laugh, the storyteller's purpose generally lies beyond mere entertainment. Stories matter. They send our kids to war. They open up our pockets. They break our hearts.

If you can uncover your character's true need for telling her story, you will have found a reason to keep telling it. When you unmask the *why*, you will find the language unspooling at your fingers. Be grateful. And go.

SEEKING STRUCTURE

> *A book is not an isolated being: it is a*
> *relationship, an axis of innumerable*
> *relationships.*
>
> —JORGE LUIS BORGES

EVERY WORK OF FICTION IS ORGANIZED
somehow—and the best of them are more pro-
foundly organized than they ever let on. Our
stories rely on the human instinct for architecture.
Structure is, essentially, a container for content. The
shape into which your story gets placed is a house
slowly built from the foundation up. Or maybe it's
a tunnel, or a skyscraper, or a palace, or even a
moving caravan, driven forward by your characters.
In fact, structure can be any number of things: you

just have to make sure that it doesn't become an elaborate hole in the ground into which we bury ourselves, unable to claw out.

Some writers try to envision the structure beforehand, and they shape the story to fit it, but this is so often a trap. You should not try to stuff your story into a preconceived structure. That, as the old expression goes, is akin to six pounds of shit wrapped in a five-pound bag.

Stories are agile things. They're elusive. They're brisk. And sometimes they're fugitive. So, the containers they go into should be pliable. You should have a grand vision, of course, an eventual endpoint, or at least the dream of an endpoint, but you must be prepared to swerve, chop and change direction at the same time. The best journeys are those where we don't exactly know what road we will take: we have a destination in mind, but the manner of getting there should be open to flux. Sometimes you have to abandon the journey altogether, retrace your footsteps, and take a different path. This is so much akin to finding a country in

which you want to live, then a province, then a
patch of land you love. On this land you want to
build a house in which you truly want to dwell. In
the creation of this structure, this house, you must
become digger, bricklayer, joiner, mason, carpenter,
plumber, plasterer, designer, tenant, owner, and, yes,
ghost in the attic too.

A proper structure mirrors the content of the
story it wants to tell. It will contain its characters
and propel them forward at the same time. And it
will generally achieve this most fully when it does
not draw too much attention to itself. Structure
should grow out of character and plot, which essentially means that it grows out of language. In
other words, the structure is forever in the process
of being shaped. You find it as you go along.
Chapter by chapter. Voice by voice. Ask yourself if
it feels right to tell the story in one fell swoop, or if
it should be divided into sections, or if it should
have multiple voices, or even multiple styles. You
stumble on through the dark, trying new things all
the time. Sometimes, in fact, you don't find the

structure until halfway through, or even when you're close to being finished. That's okay. You have to trust that it will eventually appear and that it will make sense.

The point of view will matter greatly. You might want to have a dark room in the house. A paneled library. A certain character will lead you there. He or she will give you the language to create the atmosphere: the curtains, the desk, the lamplight, the secret passage under the floorboards. The room must reflect the character. They *dwell* there. Another character will want a sunroom. Another character will want to sit, granitic, at the island in the kitchen. Others will want a circular staircase. Others are happy in the coal shed.

Just go and have a look at any house or structure that is being built in your neighborhood. Look at how bare it strikes you at first. Look at how impossible it seems that this big crate of plywood and nails and air will eventually become a place where people will love and hate each other to death. Then come back the following week. And the week after that. Allow yourself to be astounded by the physics of change. What was nothing is now something.

When it comes to structure, you will often be surprised by how mathematical the work of great writers happens to be. Don't worry. This math is a discovered thing. They didn't set out to be this way: they found it as they worked their way through. In this way, they are different from architects. They are not bound by hard-and-fast rules. They are not crimped by law. The math comes through poetry. And the poetry, then, is suspended by the math.

So, write and rearrange, write and rearrange, write and rearrange, and eventually you will begin to see the structure emerge. The harder you work, the clearer the structure will become. It will take on a shape that you recognize: a shape that never could have come simply. The difficulty had its purpose.

Now that you have a house—or an approximate one anyway—you will demolish a room here, add a turret there, rearrange a staircase down into the basement, reposition the chimney. Eventually you will have somewhere you truly want to dwell. Then you walk around the structure and add a doorway here, a wall there, trim an edge here, adjust a piece there, reorder, fix a few of the unruly angles, put the furniture in, clean the windows of all the dust.

Then you will have to invite a guest to come look around your home. The reader will not want to see the foundation, or the wiring behind the walls, or even the architectural plans. That is—and was—your work. Your secret. The reader should feel comfortable in the structure, be it palace or hut or boathouse.

Never forget that the reader nearly always moves forward in a more or less straight line through your structure, even if the writer skipped around in its creation. So put yourself in the shoes of your visitor and look around critically. Is it ambitious enough? Does it have too many windows? Have you built something that nobody has ever built before?

In the end, only you know the secrets of this

creation. Structure is the sculpture within the stone. You chisel it into life. It will eventually find its way into the museum of good storytelling. Begin with language and the content will then shape the form.

One final note: you won't have to live there forever, thank God. In this life, nobody stays in one place. You will depart the house with a hammer and nails once more.

WHAT MATTERS:
LANGUAGE AND PLOT

*Plot is, I think, the good writer's last resort
and the dullard's first choice.*

—STEPHEN KING

E TEACHERS, WE EDITORS, WE
agents, we readers, often make a mistake by
concentrating too much on plot: it is not the be-all
and end-all in a piece of literature. Plot matters, of
course it matters, but it is always subservient to
language. Plot takes the backseat in a good story
because what happens is never as interesting as *how*
it happens. And how it happens occurs in the way
language captures it and the way our imaginations
transfer that language into action. Any fat man can
come down the stairs, but only Joyce can make

stately plump Buck Mulligan descend the stairhead bearing a bowl of lather on which a mirror and a razor lie crossed.

So give me music then, young maestro, please. Make it occur the way nobody ever made it occur before. Stop time. Celebrate it. Demolish it. Slow the clock down so that the tick of each and every second lasts an hour or more. Take shotgun leaps into the past. Put backspin on your memory. Be in two or three places at one time. Destroy speed and position. Make just about anything happen. Bring back high buildings across the skyline. Unmuddy the Mississippi.

Maybe in this day and age we are diseased by plot. Let's face it, plots are good for movies, but when over-considered they tend to make books creak. So, unbloat your plot. Listen for the quiet line. Anyone can tell a big story, yes, but not everyone can whisper something beautiful in your ear. In the world of film we need motivation leading to action, but in literature we need contradiction leading to action, yes, but also leading to inaction. Nothing better than a spectacular piece of inaction. Nothing more effective than your character momentarily paralyzed by life.

The greatest novel ever written has very little apparent plot. A cuckold walks around Dublin for twenty-four hours. No shootouts, no cheap shots, no car crashes (though there is a biscuit tin launched through the air). Instead it is a vast compendium of human experience. Still, this doesn't take away from the fact that every story ever told has some sort of plot (especially *Ulysses*, which perhaps has more plot than any).

In the end, what plot must do is twist our hearts in some way. It must change us. It must make us realize that we are alive.

We must care about the music of what happens. One thing leads to the next. And the issues of the human heart unfold in front of us. Such, then, is plot. Anything can happen, even nothing at all. And even if nothing happens, the world still changes, second by second, word by word. Perhaps this is the most astounding plot of all.

PUNCTUATION:
IT'S NOT JUST A
THROWAWAY THING
(COMMA)

When I split an infinitive, God damn it, I split it so it will stay split.

—RAYMOND CHANDLER
(IN A LETTER TO HIS EDITOR)

T'S NOT A THROWAWAY THING TO TELL you the truth. It's not a throwaway thing, to tell you the truth.

Punctuation matters. In fact, sometimes it's the life or death of a sentence. Hyphens. Periods. Colons. Semicolons. Ellipses. Parentheses. They're the containers of a sentence. They scaffold your words. Should a writer know her grammar? Yes, she should. *My husband and me,* or *my husband and I*? *Their* or *they're* or *there*? *It's* or *its* or *its'*? *Where you at? I'm doing good, thanks. Toward* or *towards*? The pitfalls are just about everywhere.

Don't overuse the semicolon; it is a muscular comma when used correctly. Parentheses in fiction draw far too much attention to themselves. Learn how to use the possessive correctly as in most good writer's work. (Oops.) Never finish a sentence with an *at.* (Sorry.) Avoid too many ellipses, especially at the end of a passage, they're just a little too dramatic . . . (See?)

Grammar changes down through the years: just ask Shakespeare or Beckett or the good folks at *The New Yorker.* The language of the street eventually becomes the language of the schoolhouse. It's the difference between the prescriptive and the descriptive. And remember that if (or should we say *when*?) you are published, a copy editor will fix your grammatical errors, or at least suggest changes. So you do have a safety net of sorts.

So much depends, as William Carlos Williams

might have said, upon the red wheelbarrow—
especially if the barrow itself stands solitary at the
end of the line.

But then again, a sentence can be over-
examined. Good grammar can slow a sentence—or
indeed a wheelbarrow—down. The perfect run-
along of words can sound so stiff. Every now and
then we have to disregard the serial comma, or
leave our participles dangling, even in the rudest
way. Sometimes we make a mistake on purpose.
Perhaps knowing the difference between a main
clause and a dependent clause doesn't matter so
much so long as you can intuit the difference. You
might want to call the idea of capitalization into
question. The sentence might look better with *velcro* rather than *Velcro*, or *Hoover* rather than *hoover*.
On occasion we write a sentence that isn't, in fact,
correct, but it sings. And the question is: Would
you rather be the ornithologist or the bird?

Writers feel the grammar rather than knowing
it. This comes from good reading. If you read

enough, the grammar will come. In the end it's the language itself—the shimmyshine of it—that matters so much more than the manners the grammar police want to put upon it.

Word.

RESEARCH: GOOGLE ISN'T DEEP ENOUGH

*There are things known and there are things
unknown, and in between are the doors of
perception.*

—ALDOUS HUXLEY

RESEARCH IS THE BEDROCK OF NEARLY
all good writing, even poetry. We have to know the
world beyond our own known world. We have to
be able to make a leap into a life or a time or a geography that is not immediately ours. Often we
will want to write out of gender, race, time. This
requires deep research.

We must stretch toward the supposedly unknown. We must give ourselves access to more than
one voice. And we must do so honestly and fairly.

But how do we write about lives that are, at least on the surface, very different from our own? How can we create experiences that are imagined but true? How do we get outside of ourselves?

Some of the answer lies in proper, deep, moral research.

Yes, Google helps, but the world is so much deeper than Google. A search engine can't hold a candle to all the libraries in the world where the books actually exist, live, breathe, and argue with one another, even in the dusty basement. So go down to the library. Check out the catalogues. Go to the map division. Unlock the boxes of photographs. A librarian loves nothing more than an almost impossible question. They're the experts at finding experts.

If you want to know a life different from your own, you better try to meet it at least halfway. Get out in the street. Talk to people. Show interest. Learn how to listen. Allow your ear time to adjust. Even if you're talking about a different era, you must at least know where that era has led us. So if you want to know, say, about the life of a Hispanic shipbuilder in Florida in the 1940s, well, go to the library first, and then, if you have the chance, get down to Florida, go to a shipyard, ask around, find someone who knows someone, or someone who remembers someone, and, if not, you can still find someone in your imagination. If you try enough keys, you will eventually open a lock.

You must find the divine detail: and the more specific the detail, the better. William Gass—the American author who says quite beautifully that a writer finds himself alone with all that might happen—once suggested, while invoking Maupassant, that we should never mention an ashtray unless we are swiftly able to make it the only one in the world.

Art is a way of coping with the world by bringing it under the microscope of detail. Small intentions reveal the life of the large intentions. Most of us live in a small world anyway. And the tinier the particle, the more mysterious it is. Just ask any quark about its flavor, its color, its spin. The more mystery, the more potential for beauty. And while God is in the detail, the devil is too.

Please remember that mishandling your research is also your potential downfall. At times we can pollute our texts with too much of the obvious. It is often a good thing to have space instead so that we can fill it out with imaginative muscle. Always ask yourself, How much research is enough? Don't corrupt your texts with *facts facts facts*. Facts are mercenary things. They can be manipulated, dressed up, and shipped off anywhere. Texture is much more important than fact.

Focus in on the small detail that reveals the wider world. The key is finding the odd detail that only the experts might know. The one tiny atom that reveals the rest of the structure. Find it, use it, but don't draw too much attention to it . . . this is the magical pill of all research. Appear to be an expert, even to the experts.

The cumulative effect of your attention to detail provided by your research is what will make your stories sing.

NO RUST ON YOUR SENTENCES PLEASE

> *"I have been working hard on* Ulysses *all day," said Joyce. "Does that mean you have written a great deal?" I said. "Two sentences," said Joyce. "You've been seeking the mot juste?" "No," said Joyce, "I have the words already. What I am seeking is the perfect order of the words in the sentence."*
>
> —JAMES JOYCE WITH FRANK BUDGEN

YOU SHOULD WRITE YOUR WORK AS IF you are sending it to your reader one careful sentence at a time. Prose should be as well written as poetry. Every word matters. You must test for the rhythm and precision. Look for assonance, alliteration, rhyme. Look for internal echoes. Vary your moves. It's as close as you'll get to dancing. Listen to it create itself. Never allow it to become elevator music. It is your ability to push yourself one step further that will set you apart.

All writing deals with limits, but there should never be any sentences without at least some direction. Sail close to the wind. Be there when the bread comes out of the oven. But never forget that certain metaphors can die with overuse. No more *hot tears* please. No more *milky-white thighs*. No more dream sequences. No more *blood-red sunsets* even. No more visits to the literary souvenir shop. Instead of your character walking blandly down the road, have him jaunt, or slump, or clop, or hobble (knowing every now and then that sometimes *walk* is the perfect word).

Remember that to dress up a simple word is sometimes to take away its power. Its repetition—if repeated enough—will have the right effect. Just ask Hemingway or Chatwin or McGahern. Find the sentence that surprises you and then surprise yourself further by inserting even more surprise into it.

Put together words that nobody ever cobbled together before. This is how we achieve the unique. There are times you might spend weeks on a single sentence. Months even. No kidding.

Sometimes, in a series of spectacular sentences, insert one that is truly banal. Or within the banal, insert the spectacular. On occasion you must respect the purposeful boredom of a sentence.

Whatever you do, make it inescapably personal. Imitate, yes, but don't replicate. And imitate only to lose the original voice. Only Carver could write like Carver. Take Carver and recarve. Change those sentences which previously seemed unchangeable.

And then send those sentences to the reader you love, one envelope at a time.

THE HABIT
OF HOPING

Finding beauty in a broken world is creating beauty in the world we find.

—TERRY TEMPEST WILLIAMS

FIND YOUR LIFE—BEYOND YOUR WRITING life—worth living. Be in the habit of hoping. Allow yourself a little joy, even in the face of the world's available evidence. In fact, try to create the evidence just about anywhere you can.

THERE ARE NO LITERARY OLYMPICS

If the novel is successful, it must necessarily
be wiser than its author.

—MILAN KUNDERA

OU DON'T WRITE IN COMPETITION WITH
anyone. There are no Olympics in literature. No
gold medal, no silver, no bronze, even if the literary
awards suggest that there might be. You will soon
find out that the word *best* is not part of the true
endgame vocabulary, though the word *better* can be
accommodated. What you want to do is to write
better: it's as simple as that.

Your energies should be directed entirely at your
own work. The success or failure of others will not

make a new sentence appear from your fingertips. Just because someone else got a good review will not take away from your own possibility of a good review: it's not as if there is a limited supply. Just because they wrote a good book doesn't mean that you can't also. Just because they got a big advance doesn't mean that there is less possibility there for you.

Don't moan about other writers even if you hear them moaning about you. Let them. They'll get up at dawn with a sore throat. You, on the other hand, will have a chance to at least hit a high note or two. No need for revenge. A good sentence is revenge enough.

If you're writing to beat someone else, then you're writing with invisible ink. Watch it disappear.

Instead, keep counsel with dignity. Remain humble. Keep your gaze straight. Praise them if they deserve praise. And keep your mouth shut as much as possible if they don't.

This does not mean that you don't want to be

better than another writer—being better is part of your job. But be better in a better way. In a way that forces you into competition with yourself. Be tough and be honest. If you're going to throw a punch, try your own jaw first: get a taste of how it might feel, then walk away from it.

The most destructive force in your life is liable to be the unwritten story. If you don't write, you're not a writer. You're avoiding the competition of yourself. Simple logic, but it's a kick in the chest when the page is empty. Too much white space is not a good thing. Empty is empty. And empty haunts.

Still, don't paralyze yourself by constantly over-thinking. You can be too hard on yourself also. Know this: every writer will achieve at least one very bad book. Most of us achieve many. But even bad work is an achievement. It is not the end of the world. In fact it's the natural pattern. You still have to get up the next morning. And the morning after.

It's only for a short while that you, young writer, will have such brazen confidence as to think the morning lasts forever. It's only for a short while that you can be as optimistic as you currently are. Because, like it or not, eventually the younger writer becomes the older one, celebrating the joyful shuffle.

HOW OLD IS THE YOUNG WRITER?

> *The whole idea that people have a clue as to how the world works, is just a piece of laughable metaphysical colonialism perpetrated upon the wild country of time.*
>
> —LORRIE MOORE

OW OLD IS THE YOUNG WRITER? Seventeen, sixty, forty-six—who cares? The youngest of young writers always wants that book out before they're eighteen or at the very latest twenty-five. It's a noble ambition and not one to be scuppered, but if you don't make it, don't fret. Thirty is okay. Fifty's not bad. Sixty-four years old is as good a time as any to start: just think of

Frank McCourt. And nine years old is not bad either.

Never forget that the young writer cannot stop time. (Only in writing can we ever stop time.) Just because they're younger than you doesn't mean they will last. It's okay to put pressure on yourself— that's where your competition with yourself lies. But it's not okay to whine about it. It's not okay to start thinking that you're too old or that your time has gone. You can't give up on it. There is nothing worse than a talented writer who regrets his life, and especially one who allows that regret to knock him into silence. You can still pick up the pen long after everyone thinks that you've given up. That's the beauty of it all. You're an athlete of a different type. Your mind doesn't have to retire. So, get back to it. Resurrect it. Unfail it. Rise an hour earlier in the morning and get the work done, even secretly.

It's okay to get upset that someone else younger than you just got published. Go to the bookstore, pick up a copy, stare at their flap jacket. Dissect their bio. Whisper a very quiet curse of admiration: *Damn, she's young.* Then say: *So what?* Go home and write with a renewed fever.

And herein lies another piece of advice for a writer who might think that time has passed her by: Don't tell too many people that you're working on a book. Don't give them the chance to ask you if you've finished yet. Don't let them torture you at parties. There's almost nothing worse than the question, *How's that book of yours coming along?* (It's second to hearing that someone else has actually finished a book.) Most people don't know how long it actually takes for a book to get written. Just say *it's on its way*—even if it's not exactly on its way.

Keep working, keep shaping. Eventually it will happen. Maybe even sooner than you think.

DON'T BE A DICK

Three things in human life are important: the first is to be kind; the second is to be kind; and the third is to be kind.

—HENRY JAMES

EY, YOU. OVER THERE IN THE CORNER. Yeah, you, with that half-assed grin. Don't turn away, I know that grin, I've worn it myself. Listen up. Yeah, you. Half-listening but pretending not to. Don't get too attached to the romantic illusions of yourself. You hear me? Yeah, you over there with the tilted chin. Listen up. Save yourself from yourself.

Being a writer is not about cocaine or the White Horse Tavern or the tab of acid or the

LETTERS TO A YOUNG WRITER

Crazy Horse Saloon or the vial of laudanum or the late night of bottled-beer bravado. It's not about the hangover. Or the warehouse party. Or the jacket photo. Or the Facebook entries. Or the tweets or the twats or whatever they're called. It's not about the shirt you wear or the hat or the scarf or the white suit or any other ridiculous affectation, mea culpa. It's not about the spotlight. It's not about gloating. It's not about reaching around to slap your own back.

In the end nobody really gives a shit about the writer's life unless the writing is there first. That's all that matters. That's the endpoint. What appears on the page is what makes your life interesting.

Too many young writers think of themselves as writers rather than that which they have written. Get used to this: it must be on the page. So don't walk around thinking of yourself as a writer. Nothing worse than an author constantly obsessed with himself. Don't prop up the corner of the party with announcements about your brand new story. Don't go into workshop prattling on about your new opening salvo. Don't draw attention to any part of your life as an artist, or, even worse, an *artiste*. If someone genuinely wants to know, they will ask. Say nothing. At least until you need to say something.

Don't get me wrong: I'm not advocating a clean rap sheet or an empty liquor cabinet or prissy behavior. You don't have to live a mannered life. You don't have to be sober (but be sober while you write, please; don't fall into that trap). You don't have to be obsequious. You don't have to kowtow to anyone. You don't have to listen to older writers spouting their rubbish either. In fact, forget this letter—go, get lost, go write. Rip it up. Go write your own. See what it takes. A writer writes.

But first allow me four words of the sagest advice I know: *Don't be a dick*. At the party. In the bookstore. On the page. In your own head. Don't call people names. Don't insult your colleagues. Don't tell people how great you are. Don't drink all the wine. Don't complain that there's nobody listening. Don't ignore your friends. Don't smirk.

Don't think yourself better. Don't relegate your humility and allow it to become arrogance. Don't smoke when you're asked not to. Don't drop the silverware from the balcony. Don't gossip. Don't get sick on the carpet. Don't insult the host. Don't condescend. Don't leave your partner stranded. Don't talk about your contract. Don't mention your advance. Don't sigh. Don't yawn. Don't scratch that public itch. Don't dismiss. Don't scan the room. Don't lie. Don't fawn. Don't drop your publisher's name. Don't make a fanfare of yourself. Don't patronize. Don't humiliate. Just don't. Don't. Don't. Don't be a dick.

THEN AGAIN, DON'T BE TOO NICE (IN YOUR FICTION ANYWAY)

Don't let yourself slip and get any perfect characters . . . keep them people, people, people, and don't let them get to be symbols.

—ERNEST HEMINGWAY

APPY FAMILIES ARE ALL ALIKE, SAID Tolstoy, but every unhappy family is unhappy in its own way. So ask yourself these questions: Are you making your characters too nice? Are they too sincere? Have you given them rough edges? Have you "flawed" them up? Is there something truthful and awful (and truthfully awful) about them? Can we relate to their demons?

Our characters have to have fingerprints. Don't be afraid to push them into difficult situations. They can be mean and unreliable and racist and lonely and lost and foolish and messed up—just like the rest of us. This is, after all, real life. Or at the very least its re-creation.

And don't have your characters stand alone. Don't let them represent singular ideas. Always make sure there's something solid behind the metaphor.

As regards your own life (which really is your fiction), there are always going to be pitfalls. There will be flare-ups and divorces and the street corner brawls. Insincere words, deceit, treachery, double-dealing, and acres of bullshit to wade through. Get used to it. That's life.

It might or might not become the fuel for your stories, but the one thing is that you cannot deny it. You just keep on writing, creating life from life, rib from rib, flaw from flaw.

FAIL, FAIL, FAIL

No matter. Try again. Fail again. Fail better.
—SAMUEL BECKETT

BECKETT SAID IT BEST, AND IT DESERVES repetition over and over again: "No matter. Try again. Fail again. Fail better."

Failure is good. Failure admits ambition. Failure admits bravery. Failure admits daring. It requires courage to fail and even more courage to know that you're going to fail. Reach beyond yourself. The true daring is the ability to go to the postbox knowing that it will contain yet another rejection letter. Don't rip it up. Don't burn it. Use it as wallpaper instead. Preserve it and reread it every now and then. Know that in the years to come this rejection letter will be a piece of nostalgia. It will yellow and curl and you will remember what it once felt like to throw your words against what everyone presumed would be your silence. Failure is vivifying. You know you're better than it. Failure gets you up in the morning. Failure gets your blood circling. Failure dilates your nostrils. Failure tells you to write a bigger story and a better one.

And in the end there's only one real failure—and that's the failure to be able to fail. Having tried is the true bravery.

Take heart. Failure is a snap of sulfur to your brain. Light a match. Inhale.

READ, READ, READ

> *Trying to write without reading is like venturing out to sea all by yourself in a small boat: lonely and dangerous. Wouldn't you rather see the horizon filled, end to end, with other sails? Wouldn't you rather wave to neighboring vessels; admire their craftsmanship; cut in and out of the wakes that suit you, knowing that you'll leave a wake of your own, and that there's enough wind and sea for you all?*
>
> —TÉA OBREHT

YOU WOULD BE AMAZED BY THE NUMBER of writers who just do not read, especially older writers who believe that they are the only ones who

deserve to be read. Their reading world shrinks.
They believe that they have written enough that
they can afford now to come indoors. They close
the curtains. They deposit themselves in the corners
of the couch, shadowed by their bookshelves. They
dip in for a few pages and find themselves
exhausted. They sell their curiosity to the sound of
their own words. They forget about finding the
expansive in others. But forgive them, forgive me.
We have forgotten what it meant to be a young
writer.

So here it is, before I forget again. A young
writer must read. She must read and read and read.
Adventurously. Promiscuously. Unfailingly. It
sounds so simple. Yet it is not. Not even the simpli-
fication of it. She must read everything that comes
her way. The classics, the old books that speak to
her from the shelves, the tomes recommended by
teachers, the chapbooks left on the subway seats,
the old dog-eared novels in the railway station, the
ancient hardcover in the holiday cottage. Read,
read, read. The brain is an agile canister. Your mind

can contain so much. The more difficult the book, the better. The greater the agility of your reading, the greater the elasticity of your own work.

Challenge yourself. Get out of the comfort zone. Find something that confounds others. The great joy in difficulty is, in fact, its difficulty.

A young writer must also read her contemporaries. Fiercely and jealously. She must go into the bookshop and spend hours in awe and contemplation. She must flip to the biographies at the back. She must get her blood boiling. *Shit, that author comes from my hometown. How dare they say what I want to say?* Yes, rage, but a temporary rage. Not in competition, but in desire. (After all, they are not taking your job: your job is entirely your own, nobody else can have it, who else is going to finish your piece of literary carpentry, unless it's an Ikea chair?)

A young writer must go to the library and wander through the dusty old stacks. Run your fingers along the shelf. Follow your instincts. It is amazing how a book will find you. There is somehow a homing device in language. Unlike love, there is a destined one always there. And it can be found at any time. You must be open to it. Then you open it up to its magnitude of suggestion. The world is suddenly cleaved open.

You read to fire your heart aflame. You read to lop the top of your head off. You read because you're the bravest idiot around and you're willing to go on an adventure into the joy of confusion. You know when a book is working. Give it time.

And if it confuses you while thrilling you, that's a good sign, keep going, keep going, keep going. Absolute consistency is unimaginative. Confusion is an honest response. Change comes about because of confusion. But there also comes a time when you might have to throw it away. Life is too short to drink bad wine, but it's shorter still when it comes to bad books. So be prepared to jettison that book, but only after you have given it a good chance.

A good book will turn your world sideways. It will also turn your own writing inside out. The prose writers should read the poets. The poets should read the novelists. The playwrights should read the philosophers. The journalists should read the short story writers. The philosophers should read through the entire crew. In fact, we all should read the entire crew. Nobody makes it alone.

I have heard young writers say that they don't have time to read. That's most likely because they have already taken too much time shooting their mouths off. Listen, young writer, it's ridiculous to say you don't have the time to open a book. It's ludicrous to claim that a book is too long. It's unimaginative not to try the hardest work available. Márquez. Woolf. Gaddis. Hansen. Gass. This is the past shaping your future. It's in what you read. We get our voices from these books. We discover masters this way and then we shape our own form of mastery by imitating, echoing, journeying through the canyon toward the canon, or the cannon—or both.

But if you don't read—especially in the direction of that which is supposedly difficult—you will never sustain your own writing. So, go. Rip up this damn letter. Find a corner. Open a book. Read the hardest thing you possibly can.

Joan Didion says that we tell ourselves stories in order to live. So, live as many lives as you can. Over and over and over again.

REJOYCE

REJOICE. READ JOYCE.

WRITING IS ENTERTAINMENT

> *In dark times, the definition of good art would seem to be art that locates and applies CPR to those elements of what's human and magical that still live and glow despite the times' darkness.*
>
> —DAVID FOSTER WALLACE

NEVER FORGET THAT ART IS ENTERtainment. It is your duty to reflect the world, yes, but it's also your duty to bring a bit of brightness to it too.

Hang a Nietzsche quote up on your wall: We have art, he says, so we shall not die of too much reality.

Go down to the dark places, but bring a flaming

torch. We have to have light enough to see the page. Make it colorful. Make it funny. Don't remain stuck on one note. Shake it up. We have to keep ourselves open to all possibilities. Be interested in any available joy. The best writing makes us sit up and take notice and it makes us glad that we are— however briefly—alive.

TAKE A BREAK

Anything can happen, the tallest towers be overturned, those in high places daunted.

—SEAMUS HEANEY

E VERY NOW AND THEN, TAKE A BREAK. Go on holiday. Leave everything but the notebook behind. Learn how to like writing again. Miss it for a week or so. Don't fret. Guess what: that blank page isn't going anywhere.

WHO'S YOUR IDEAL READER?

> *If we're lucky, writer and reader alike, we'll*
> *finish the last line or two of a short story and*
> *then just sit for a minute, quietly.*
>
> —RAYMOND CARVER

ULTIMATELY YOUR IDEAL READER IS you. You are the one who has to take responsibility for it in the end. You must be prepared to listen to the deepest, most critical part of yourself. When you write something, try to imagine yourself a couple of decades from now, reading over the same piece, wondering if it still has worth. See yourself with a bit of time under your belt. Will your story stand up to the scrutiny of the new you? Will it embarrass you? Will it send a shiver of cold along

your spine? Will you think, *Did I do the right thing?*
Will you think, *Did I hurt people?*

Be kind to yourself as well as being tough.
Remember that any fool can knock a house down;
it takes a real craftsperson to have built it in the
first place.

HOW TO GET AN AGENT

> *One of the few things I know about writing*
> *is this: spend it all, shoot it, play it, lose it, all,*
> *right away, every time. . . . Give it, give it*
> *all, give it now.*
>
> —ANNIE DILLARD

F I HAD A DOLLAR FOR EVERY TIME I'VE
been asked how to get an agent, I wouldn't have to
have an agent. Do you need an agent? Yes, yes, and
(most of the time) yes. Finding one isn't all that difficult, but finding the right one can change your
life.

First of all, find a writer whose work you admire. A younger one, preferably. Someone who is

already represented by an agency, but is on the cusp of making an even greater success of their career. Find out who their agent is. It's easily done—it's the magic of Google, or the acknowledgments page, or trawling through a few website interviews. Then write the agent a letter or an email. Be quick and expansive both. Tell them you like their stable of writers and one in particular who seems to open up the airways of literature. Give them a little background, who you are, where you went to school, what you've already published. Ask if they'd like to read a few pages. Boast a little if you want. Strut your stuff. That's all right. Agents are used to it. (Always tell them that you're working on a novel . . . even if you're not working on a novel yet.) Be smart, be confident, and always be brief.

If they write back—and don't expect anybody to write back—please don't celebrate yet. Call them, talk to them, visit them, check them out. Ask them questions. The most important thing you should know about an agent is that you employ them, they don't employ you. Some of them may make you feel (especially at the beginning of your career) that they have you in a tight harness, but the truth of the matter is that freedom is feeling easy in the harness.

A good agent doesn't lay down the law. Rather, they allow the law to unfold. They make business decisions. They ease the tax implications. They chat with editors and publishers and reporters. They forward invitations. They cull some of the loony tunes who might want to get in touch with you. They get you gigs. They talk you up. Yes, they can change your life instantly. And, yes, they can show you the money. But essentially you are your own agent, because the only thing it comes down to is the language on the page.

You should be the governor of your own writing. Don't change your words to suit an agent unless you know—deep in your heart's core—that the agent is correct. Even then you must make sure that you are not compromising yourself. This is your work, after all. Agents become agents because they want things to sell, not necessarily to sing (although a great agent will sell and sing simultaneously).

Listen to the agent, but be the agent of your own agency. This takes deep intuition. And a bit of style. And a good dose of humility.

Don't forget that you will be paying your agent anywhere up to twenty percent of your money, so a good agent will get you at least twenty-five percent more than you even imagined. Pay this willingly. Don't question their expense sheet. Don't second-guess them. Don't whine or whisper. Your agent should be on your side. If he is not, then remember that you are his employer and fire him. Excuse me? Fire him, I said, fire him. (But not until you've found another agent.)

Remember that this is *your* work. You go to the coalface every day. You know what it takes to lift that bucket of words up from the well. Be true to this instinct. You know where true value lies. Your words should jangle, not just your pocket.

Now, go write.

WHAT IF I DON'T GET AN AGENT?

The way to despair is to refuse to have any kind of experience.

—FLANNERY O'CONNOR

B UT WHAT IF I DON'T GET AN AGENT? Don't despair. Write on. Keep your arse in the seat. Get the words down on the page. Do what you love. Fight. Persevere. Find the magazines and journals you like. Go to the contributors list. Find the name of the editor. Then find his or her email address. Write a letter, a personal letter, a heartfelt letter, something with personality and style. Ask if they would like to read your work. Don't be afraid. Be polite. Be humble. Be kind. And yet triumph yourself at the same time. The only thing you can lose here is a few words or a few minutes of an email. Send it out and then forget it. Get on with the next thing. Don't sit around, don't obsess, don't shadow the phone, don't hover over the mouse. Don't even hope. You've already done the big thing by finishing.

Guess what? Nothing wrong with being rejected. It happens to everyone. (I have wallpapered bathrooms with rejection slips.) Try it again a few months later. Don't get wounded. Don't be temperamental. Have a sense of humor. Remind them that they once sent you a fabulously written rejection letter. And to hell with simultaneous submissions! Pepper-spray the magazines you love! Send, send, send! Whoever accepts you first wins the prize. But don't play magazines off one another. Don't bargain or trade.

Go to the postbox every day and accept that the bad news will eventually make the good news feel even better. An agent will eventually come knocking. Or a publisher will come knocking. (They do read even the smallest magazines, by the way.)

Be daring. Be original. Nothing good is ever achieved through predictability.

FINDING THE RIGHT EDITOR

I can't write without a reader. It's precisely like a kiss—you can't do it alone.

—JOHN CHEEVER

A GREAT EDITOR IS A PRECIOUS thing. Maybe it's your best friend. Maybe it's a classmate. Maybe it's a workshop participant. Maybe it's your husband. Maybe it's someone you hire. Or maybe it's the editor at a magazine or publishing house. No matter what, the right editor has to be someone you trust. You have to give them space. You have to give them time. You have to listen. You have to be humble in the presence of their opinion. Simple as it sounds, you have to respect them. You don't always have to agree with them.

It's about your own ability to see someone else re-shaping your work. But it's also about their ability to be wrong. Assess the value of what they say. Try the sentence with their edit. Try it without. Speak it aloud. Say it again. Thank them for the edit, even if you didn't use it.

If you're in the lucky position that your book or story has sold, remember that the editor who acquired it is not a box to be ticked off. She can be the sculptor of your writing. Be thankful when the suggestions arrive. And remember she does so much more than editing. She negotiates your deal. She gets your books sent out for blurbs. She goes to marketing meetings. She watches you get the praise, and gets little herself. And, if you don't get the praise, she suffers.

An editor is a person who knows what the limelight is and has chosen to shadow it. Acknowledge that shadow.

And every now and then send her flowers out of the blue.

BRINGING (YOUR OWN) FRESH EYES TO YOUR STORIES

All that I hope to say in books, all that I ever hope to say, is that I love the world.

—E. B. WHITE

WRITING CAN EXHAUST US. SOMEtimes we just can't see the words anymore. We have become so close that we forget what it might be like to read it for the first time. Often we need a bit of breathing space between us and our work.

When you've finished a story or a poem, try putting it away for a week or two so that you can look at it with fresh eyes. Write something else for a while. Believe in absence. Enjoy the loneliness.

When you are rested and ready to get reacquainted with your work, do so with joy and trepidation both. Title it. Give it an epigraph. Print it out. Bind it up. Tuck it under your arm. Go out somewhere public. Assert that your work exists beyond your own mind. Go into the streets. Find a park bench or a coffee shop or a library where you can sit down with it. Pretend you are a brand new reader who has never seen these pages before. Be surprised, even by the sight of your own name on the front page. Go from beginning to end, stopping only to scrawl an odd note in the margin. Be honest with yourself. Is it something that still thrills you? Has it taken on the right shape? Is it something you can take home and continue? Have you breathed air into its lungs? Has the heart grown fonder?

Or is it time to throw it away?

THROW IT ALL AWAY

> *One does not discover new lands without*
> *consenting to lose sight of the shore for a*
> *very long time.*
>
> —ANDRÉ GIDE

SOMETIMES, YOUNG WRITER, YOU JUST have to have the *cojones* to wipe the whole slate clean.

Occasionally you know—you know, you just *know,* deep in your gut—that it's not good enough. Or you've been chasing the wrong story. Or you've been slogging through the tar long enough. Or you've been waiting for another moment of inspiration. You've been hanging on but the truth of it is that you're down to your last fingernail.

Often the true voice is not heard until long into the story. It might be a year of work, hundreds of pages, or even more. (One of the most liberating days of my writing life was when I threw eighteen months of work away.) But something in you knows—it just knows—that everything you have written so far has just been preparation for what you are now about to write. You have finally found your north, your east, your west. No south, no going back.

So you have to throw it away.*

It is terrifying of course. You close the file, you bury the pages. You have a little wake for the words. You whiskey them up. But part of this—like any wake—is celebration too. The deep knowledge is that every bit of work you've done has led you to

---

* Okay, let's be honest here: you don't actually throw the pages away. Box them up or back them up, put a toe tag on them and keep them somewhere within reach, just in case you might be making a mistake. And someday you might go back to them and find a gem of a sentence here, or the germ of an idea there. But you have to mentally throw them away, at least for a little while, while the new story takes root.

this point. You have created a sort of muscular memory. You have been writing toward your obsession, but now you have found the point where that obsession will truly open up. Be thankful. Your thrown-away pages have led you here. Your work has served its purpose.

Now you're pageless and your back is truly up against the wall. A little bit of sympathy from friends can help, but only for a day or two while you cultivate that secret rage that every writer knows: you have to write, simple as that.

So you open up another file, sharpen the pencil, and settle down once again.

ALLOW THE READER'S INTELLIGENCE

*Good writing is supposed to evoke sensation
in the reader—not the fact that it is raining,
but the feeling of being rained upon.*

—E. L. DOCTOROW

ONE OF THE GREAT RULES OF WRITING classes is "Show, don't tell." What this means is that you must guide a reader through unfamiliar territory without taking away the experience, the living moments of the story. We read in order to inhabit newness. Move the reader physically through a story. Guide them. And then surprise them once more.

Try not to say too much in your story or your poem or anywhere else for that matter. Never dictate. (Alas, he dictates.) Avoid pointing out what your stories mean. Trust your reader. Allow the revelation to belong to them. You are a guide in a foreign land. Be kind, but not too kind.

When you allow your reader their intelligence, they will come back to you again and again and again. Challenge. Confront. Dare. Cleave open new territory. Even confuse them. Then let them go. Say just enough that they can learn the territory for themselves. In this way you're always a step or two ahead of your reader but even the best of them don't actually know it. Good stories are written, in the end, by their readers.

SUCCESS

I would rather give full vent to all human
loves and disappointments, and take a chance
on being corny, than die a smartass.

—JIM HARRISON

I F AT FIRST YOU DO SUCCEED, BE ENTIRELY astonished. Then convince yourself that you will never be able to do it again. The magic of success lies in the proximity and impossibility of the unattainable. And if you do continue to succeed, be wary, be very very wary. The only guarantee is that it won't always happen.

Success, too, has the arc of a story: it will end. To some this is a terrifying thing, but to the properly successful person, it is the only ecstasy.

IF YOU'RE DONE, YOU'VE ONLY JUST BEGUN

Have regrets. They are fuel. On the page they flare into desire.

—GEOFF DYER

JUST BECAUSE YOU'VE TYPED THE LAST sentence—remember, bloodstains are far more visible than tears—doesn't mean that you've actually finished a book. A book might take a few years to write, but even after it's written it still has to be finished. Patience and tenacity, please. Patience, I said. Patience. Writing is about seventy-five percent of the job. There's the editing. And then there's the editing. Oh, and then there's the editing. And, after that, there's the editing again. After that there's the copyediting. Then there's the publicity meeting.

And then there's the marketing meeting. Then there's some more editing. Then there's the request for blurbs. Then there's a proof copy. Then there's the final editing. A tweak here, a tweak there. Then there's the wait. The pause. The hold. The catch of breath. The wish that you had edited more.

Then there are the op-eds that you hope to place at the very least in *The New York Times*. Then there's the wailing and gnashing of teeth when the op-ed appears in an online journal read by only six people. But, hey, that's six more readers than before. Then you wait some more.

You lie awake at night. Then there's the visit to the seventh circle of hell: the first reviews. Don't despair too much. Don't rejoice too much either. You are only halfway through. Then, a month or so before publication, the first six copies come in the post. Take one out of the box. Cherish it. Give it a drink. Give yourself a drink too. Dance around your apartment. Knock over the shelves. Tuck the book away as the first copy you ever touched. Give out other copies to your loved ones: your partner, your mother, your friends who supported you all along. Buy at least twenty more first editions. Yes, you have to buy them, believe it or not. There are no endless free books. But you should get them half-price. Or your editor might sling a box of them your way.

Do not give all your first editions away. Repeat, *do not give them all away.* Tuck away five or six of them for you, your kids, your grandkids, and others you love. Hopefully, there will be many more editions in the future. Trust me, you don't want to end up paying for a first edition of your first ever book. Hopefully, it will be good enough that readers will want it forever. So it sits on your shelf. And then you get ready for the onslaught. You pray that at least some of it comes.

You have your first reading. You do a small book tour. You find some kindred spirits. A lot of the time you go out to silence. That's the toughest thing of all. This thing that you have worked on for years, nobody seems to give a damn. But so what? Good writers have stamina. Good writers have perseverance. Good writers have desire. You get back up and you begin again.

Even better, you have begun your second book long before the first comes out. You have kindled that fire, and the disappointment of the ash-heaped first doesn't even matter. And if you find—as you should—that the second book is harder than the first, then you are the writer that you always wanted to become.

BLURBS (OR THE ART OF LITERARY PORN)

Thank you for the manuscript. I shall lose no time in reading it.

—BENJAMIN DISRAELI

BLURBS ARE THE PUBLISHED WRITER'S nightmare. Either he gives them to other writers or he doesn't. If he doesn't, he's an arsehole. If he does, he's an arsehole too—unless he blurbs yours, whereupon he is an angel, a godsend, a creature divine.

But how do you get a blurb in the first place? You beg, you plead, you cajole. You ask your editor to put her heart on the line. Have her reach out to her stable of writers. She might find someone who likes your voice, someone you can align with. She

might even know the phone number of the blurb
whore: there are a few of us around, some of us
getting a little bit tired (me too, Mr. Shteyngart!
ahoy! the exclamation mark! the red lantern of
blurbdom!). Ask your agent too, he's got the phone
numbers too. But guess what? Not much is going
to happen. Forgive my blatant cynicism. But a lot
of the time you're going to have to do the legwork
yourself. Go to the writers you know and admire.
Write them a personal note. Be sincere and genu-
ine, of course, but be creative too. Write a letter
that crackles. One that shoots electricity along all
its lines. One they can't ignore. (Though they most
likely will ignore it—in fact, never ever ever ever
expect a reply: some overly generous writers can get
twenty or more requests a week, no kidding, ask
Gary, he gets twenty-one, sometimes twenty-two,
his postman hates him.) Never forget that it takes
at least two or three days for anyone to properly
read a novel. That's a lot of time and energy from
someone who's trying to make ends meet.

If you hear back from them, do a backflip. If

they read your work, triple somersault. If they actually blurb it, book a ticket for at least the nearest satellite. But if they don't blurb it, don't worry. And don't hold a grudge. Half the time they don't even open the mail, mea culpa once again. The rest of the time they are busy chasing blurbs of their own; it's a back scratcher's world.*

A lot of good writers don't ask for blurbs anymore, precisely because they don't have the time to give them. So if you fail with an author you admire, don't disappear down to the river to drown. There are other ways to stay afloat. If you went to an MFA program, you go back to old teachers and you *plámás* them until they accede. (*Plámás*—a wonderful Irish word for "flattery designed to bend people

---

* "Colum McCann's chapter on blurbing is full of shimmering heartbreak matched only by an angry lucidity and a peerless semicolon. It is an essential guide not just to how we blurb but to *why* we blurb. This is a blurb chapter writer to watch. Not since Joyce has an Irishman written about blurbing with such brio and quintessential Ulysses-ness. Blurb chapter prize committees, lay down your other chapters. You have a winner right here."

—GARY SHTEYNGART,
AUTHOR OF *A-BLURB-ISTAN*

to your will.") If you didn't go to an MFA program, find one nearby and ask the writers there. Or go to someone in your writing group who has already published a novel. Word of advice: make it as easy as possible for them and, if necessary, even offer your own dream blurb in "their" voice that they can then edit and shape. It's a terrible truth, but some writers only read a portion of the books they blurb, if even that.

A blurb is pure fluffery. It's a form of literary porn. Most readers know they're being fluffed.

The truth is that blurbs are not for readers anyway. It's an in-house argument for publishers. They're for the sales force in your company. And for the bookshops who buy advance copies. They're for the purpose of the pitch. It's so your book can get positioned on the shelves by your favorite bookseller. It's a not-so-subtle whisper in the advance reviewer's ear.

So, it's all a bit of a shell game, yes. But when the good blurb comes, the truly generous one, the one that captures the essence of your book, it's not a blurb anymore, it's a shout-out, it's a violin note, it's a drum crash, it's a barbaric yawp across the rooftops of literature that you have written something that has got under the skin of another. Cherish it. Enjoy the feeling.

Soon you will be writing them.

A SECRET HEARING

No need to hurry. No need to sparkle. No need to be anybody but oneself.

—VIRGINIA WOOLF

OFTEN, IN THE MIDST OF A NOVEL OR a story, you'll be surprised to realize that you have little or no idea where you are going. You're operating on the fumes of the language and the vague feeling that what you are doing will eventually have texture and depth. It's a deep-sea dive without very much training or equipment, but suddenly, a few feet down, you hit upon a word or an image and you realize with a start that this is the path you were meant to take. You don't know why. You don't know where. You don't even know how. It is a form of astounded hearing, a secret listening. You have made a daring raid on the inarticulate. This feeling has its own energy. You have to follow it. You'd be a fool if you didn't at least pursue the sentence in whatever direction it is taking you.

It's like solving a perplexing question in deep-sea physics: Why was I allowed to come to such a depth? There is a moment when the solution is so simple and evident that you wonder why you hadn't come upon it before: when, like Archimedes, you notice the bathwater suddenly rise. You know what you have found, what you've been seeking for years.

The simplicity of it is stunning simply because it seemed so difficult in the beginning. Now it is there. It has appeared. Somehow the inarticulate has been ransacked. It exists because writing is about trying to achieve a fundamental truth that everybody knows is there, but nobody has quite yet located.

Follow it.

WHERE SHOULD
I WRITE?

Build your own cabin and piss off the front
porch whenever you bloody well feel like it.

—EDWARD ABBEY

WRITERS WRITE JUST ABOUT EVERY-
where. In ships. On trains. In libraries. On the subway. In cafés. In writers' retreats. On top of fridges.
In plush offices. In jail cells. In the hearts of
hollowed-out trees. There's a good deal of shite
talked about writers in their garrets (I sometimes
work in a closet, for crying out loud), wearing
blindfolds to block out the world, but it doesn't
really matter where you write as long as you feel
comfortable there.

Still, a book will reflect the room in which it is

written, so make it comfortable, make it intimate, make sure you belong there, that the space is yours. What helps? A good chair, of course: spend your money on this. A decent posture. A few feet to stretch in every now and then. A couple of photographs (maybe one of your characters as you imagine them, or the landscape she dwells in). Or a favorite quote—"No Matter"—tacked up on the wall. A pencil? Yes. A pen? Yes. A typewriter? Yes. A computer? Yes. A tape recorder? Yes, if that's your style. Maybe all of the above: it doesn't matter how you write, it's *what* you write. But if you have a computer, try to make sure you have a way to guillotine the Internet. Best of all have no Internet whatsoever. Try not to smoke. Try not to have a drink at least until the end of the working day. Keep your favorite volume of poetry handy. Write advice to yourself in a notebook or on the wall. Try not to eat in your workspace: crumbs attract other dwellers.

Avoid writing in bed and even avoid your bedroom if possible: why spend all your dreams in one room? Enjoy the generosity of others. If someone offers a cabin, take it. Sit by the ocean or sit by the lake. You don't necessarily need a window but sometimes it helps. Get out and about. Take a walk. Allow yourself to be lost. Follow a trail deep into the distance.

If you think it will help, go to the writers' colony (what a strange word, *colony,* it suggests the tinkle of ice somewhere, or the presence of birds, or indeed the arrival of ants). Go there with purpose. Be generous to the other writers, but hide away from them while you write. Your book is the only book. Close your door. Turn your phone off. It is your time to be selfish. Let others pay the bills. Let others worry about the dog for a while. Escape. Take your clothes off. Dance around. Play music. If you have a favorite writing album—buy *And Now the Weather* by Colm Mac Con Iomaire—put it on auto-repeat so that the music seeps into the background and becomes then part of the landscape of your language. Keep the room a little cold: this will preserve the wakefulness in you.

And when you have finished a book, or a story, change your desk around a little, put up new photographs, tack new pictures on the wall, move the world, undust yourself.

Here it is: a room with another view.

TO MFA OR
NOT TO MFA?

It is dangerous to live in a secure world.

—TEJU COLE

AND WHAT ABOUT THAT MFA WRITing program? The truth is that nobody can teach you how to write. A program might *allow* you to write, but it will not *teach* you. But allowing is the best form of teaching anyway.

So, go to the MFA program if it feels right, but don't expect some writer to solve it all for you. Go there to mess up. Go there to find a safe place to fail. Go there to find a community of readers. Go there because you will get a chance to breathe amongst others who are learning the exact same art. A single word in a workshop might knock six months off your writing curve. Be patient. It is an apprenticeship. It is likely to frustrate you at first. In fact workshop can be one of the most humiliating experiences of a writer and even a teacher's life. In the end of the program (or the pogrom), you might be more mystified than ever before. That's okay. This too will settle. Give it time. Often a lesson is not properly heard until years later anyway.

A couple of words of advice—don't go straight out of college. Give yourself a year or two to live your life. And live it out loud. Live it dangerously. That way you will have something to write about. You will destroy the blank page when it stares back at you.

Young writer, listen please: Avoid the bloated MFA programs that charge fifty grand (yes, fifty grand!) a year in order to saddle you with a back-alley classroom and a second-rate teacher. A good deal of the time these programs are a final resort for washed-up poets and novelists. (Then again they might be good teachers for that very reason:

they have been through the mill and they might guide you away.) But whatever you do, don't go to an MFA program to impress your great-aunt Gertrude, the Ivy League queen. Go where the words matter.

Research the program carefully. Find the place that fits. A landscape that suits you. Students who suit you. Be aware of who will be your teacher. And be wary of what they promise. Make a commitment to your work, but don't forget that part of being at an MFA program is that you will be working with at least a dozen other young writers: you will have to be selfish and selfless both.

In the end you are the one who will do all the learning. The fact of it is that there is no school but your own school. (I got rejected by all but one of the MFA programs I applied to, and in the end I just wrote on my own. I'm not interested in using the rejection as a badge of honor, however—I know I would have learned things quicker if I had gone to an MFA.) Still, you don't have to go to an MFA program in order to learn how to write. Did I say this already? Writers write. They position themselves on their arses and they . . . write.

So, revere the cabin in the woods if that's where you end up. Revere the long days of silence and shuffle in the shithole apartment. Revere the fellowship. Revere poverty. Revere the inheritance. Revere whatever path you take. In the end nothing will matter but the actual words upon the page: who cares if they came from an MFA or not?

Find yourself a person who knows these things, be it colleague, friend, or even enemy. Find a teacher. Give him or her a break. The best teacher will know that she is not teaching you at all.

What is there to do, then? Be guided by others who have failed—and failed willingly—before you. Be generous to their failings. Most of the time they did not get it right themselves. But they just might get it right for you.

SHOULD I READ WHILE I'M WRITING?

> *Read the greatest stuff, but read the stuff that isn't so great, too. Great stuff is very discouraging. If you read only Beckett and Chekhov, you'll go away and only deliver telegrams at Western Union.*

> —EDWARD ALBEE

I'T'S HARD TO SAY WHAT YOU SHOULD BE reading while you're writing, but I will say this: At the start of a novel, you should be reading as widely and voraciously as you can. The writing can go anywhere and you are likely to be inspired by whatever you read. You are preparing to migrate. Reading at this stage will only help the lift-off.

Toward the middle of a project, your reading

should be more directed, more focused, more in the vein of proper research. You are on fire now, you are moving. The prose writers should try some poetry, and the poets should be steeping themselves in some prose.

Toward the end of a novel, you should be thinking of turning your bookshelves around, throwing away the library key, fleeing the cage. At this stage you are pure flight, pure motion, pure wing. Your story has only one purpose—and that's to find where it is that it will land.

At this point, you do not need any other writer whispering in your ear. You will intuit this landing space in the silence of your own head, and generally not by reading others. This is not to say that you won't find inspiration elsewhere, but make sure the elsewhere is suitably distant. At this juncture, read away from your discipline.

But what happens if you discover that, after all is said and done, someone seems to be writing the same story as you, or that it is already signed, sealed, and delivered? As long as you are sure you didn't consciously plagiarize it, don't worry. Seriously. No two stories are ever the same. None. None whatsoever. In fact the only one likely to know about this possible repetition is you.

Stories are not about plot, they are about language and rhythm and music and style. If you believe in your own story, and write it well, it will find its readers. Good work will endure. Just don't make the mistake of becoming a pale carbon copy of someone else. Be careful when transcribing your notes. Make sure that the words are yours. But let's not forget that our voice has come from somewhere else and nothing is ever truly unique. So if you are compared to another writer, bow your head, blush, be thankful, and move on. And, please, if you did unconsciously make a mistake, and echoed a line, acknowledge it. No excuses. No stammering. It's a big language but every now and then it's going to repeat itself.

The only thing that should surround a good line is another good line. This is how you carve your voice.

SMASH THAT MIRROR

Nothing factual that I write or say will be as truthful as my fiction.

—NADINE GORDIMER

WRITING FICTION CAN HURT PEOPLE. In fact, it can shatter them. It doesn't matter so much if it hurts just you alone, but if it begins to hurt others, especially those near and dear to you, you should smash that mirror you're staring into.

Stop writing about yourself. Don't steal directly from your friend's life. Don't write about your father's woes. Don't use your girlfriend's body for literary cartography. Don't use your boyfriend's neuroses to bleed out an extra paragraph. Don't take events from what some call *real life* and then transcribe them to the page. There's nothing heroic about stripping your friends or family down in front of your own eyes, even if it is literary.

If you're writing a novel, get out of your own head and into the bigger world. Invent the neuroses, invent the cartography, invent the woes. Create a new father in which your own father can be embedded. Change the name. Change the face. Change the time. Change the weather. It will be a relief. Your father will then emerge full and alive, but unrecognizable, allowed freedom to exist in an entirely new body. In fact he will probably have more depth. So too will your own life.

Of course there are notable exceptions. Maybe you're a journalist. Maybe you're a social historian. Maybe you're Karl Ove Knausgaard. Maybe you're that poet who believes that his life is there to be written upon. Maybe you think you matter more than you truly do. But what's the point in excavating your family when you have in your power the ability to create a whole new family alongside your own?

And don't expect—even in fiction—for written things to be true just because they happened. This is no excuse. They have to happen on the page. With rhythm. With style. With a fierce honesty that is true to experience, not to fact.

All writing is imagination. It creates out of dust. Even what they choose to call *nonfiction*.

In the end imagination is a form of memory-making. Use it. What we're talking about here is a responsibility to freedom. This is not about avoidance. It's about a much deeper truth that lies within you, but you maybe haven't yet acknowledged.

Trust me, if you stop writing directly about yourself you will feel liberated. Everything you know will end up inside everything you have imagined. Your characters will be far more true when they are freed by creative intent.

When you supposedly avoid yourself, you will have only done one thing, a great paradox: you will have written yourself. And you're the only one you can, or should, damage.

From this, then, you can go on and re-create.

THE DARK DOGS OF
THE MIND

> *I haven't found a drug yet that can get you*
> *anywhere near as high as sitting at a desk*
> *writing.*

> —HUNTER S. THOMPSON

DEPRESSION IS AN OCCUPATIONAL
hazard, young writer. But don't wallow in it. Don't
become fossilized in despair. Don't paralyze yourself in the aspic of gloom. If you stare into the
abyss long enough, it will stare out from you. The
unexamined life may not be worth living, but the
over-examined life can be soul crushing too.

So, don't shirk your responsibility to find some
sort of meaning, no matter how dark. All good

books are about death in one form or another. Celebrate it. Find where it intersects with life.

Allow the act of the imagination to revive you. Write to outdistance yourself from misery. Write so the world doesn't close in upon you. Write so you eventually open new directions.

All of this is not to outright refuse or even refute the idea of depression. It happens, sure, but please don't succumb to it completely. Dig your characters out of the ice in which your reality has encased them. More than anything, you will be digging yourself out too.

WRITE YOURSELF
A CREDO

There is no agony like bearing an untold story inside you.

—ZORA NEALE HURSTON

SIT DOWN—RIGHT NOW!—RIGHT now!—and write yourself a credo.* What is it that you believe in? What is it that you want to do with your writing? Who is it that you want to speak to? What is your relationship with language? How, if at all, do you want to see the world shifted? Continue wanting to know what it is that you want to know. Try this at different times of your career. Maybe even try for a credo every single year, or at least one every five years. Keep them together.

Watch yourself flourish—or not. And if not, why not? Why not? That's a credo in itself.

---

*   A Credo for 2017: At certain points in history it is only the poetic that is capable of dealing with brute reality. You arrive at the conjunction of these two forces—reality and fiction—and make a decision about how to proceed. There you stand, on the edge of two tectonic plates. What you have to do, then, is let the facts go. Let the figures go. Let the simplicities disappear. Let the sound bites drown. Descend into language instead. Fight the abyss. (C McC)

THE BUS THEORY

You must write as if the very fate of the world depends upon it.

—ALEKSANDAR HEMON

MAYBE THE BEST WAY TO GAUGE THE true importance of what you're doing is the Bus Theory. You wake up in the morning. You get to your workspace. You concentrate. You dig. You create.

At the end of the workday—be it an hour, or a morning, or the whole livelong day—you walk out into the world. The traffic slides by in the street. The world is its ordinary self. You still carry your quiet sentences with you. A little distracted, you step off the curb. Suddenly there's a whoosh of air, a blast of horn, a whack of diesel, a scream. The bus misses you by inches. Less than inches. A whisker away. It's not so much that your life passes before your eyes, but your novel does, your poem does, your story does. You step back onto the street and catch your breath. You know, like everyone knows, that you do not ever want to be hit by a bus, but if you *are* to be sideswiped—if the world *is* fated that way—then the bus must at the very least wait until your book is completed. *If I have to go, Lord, please allow me the dignity of writing my last sentence.*

This Bus Theory—which might also be called the Theory of Purpose—will help get you out of bed in the morning. It proves the value of your struggle. The work matters. The story needs to be told.

Death is not an option, at least for now.

WHY TELL STORIES?

*Storytelling is an escape from the jail of the
self, leading to the ultimate adventure—
seeing life through the eyes of another.*

—TOBIAS WOLFF

WHY DO WE TELL STORIES? WHY DO
we have a deep need to *tell* one another that which
is real and invented both? Why do we need to lean
across the table, or the fireside, or the fabulously in-
tertwined wires of the Internet, and whisper "Listen"? We do it because we're sick of reality and we
need to create what isn't yet there.

Stories and poems create what is yet to come.
A sentence spun from the imagination is a
powerful embrace of what is new. Literature

proposes possibilities and then makes truths of them. In storytelling we are given some of the most profound evidence of being alive.

The word *fiction* really means to shape or to mold. It derives from the Latin *fictio* and the verb is *fingere* and the past participle, interestingly, is *fictus*. It does not (necessarily) mean to lie, or to invent. It doesn't mean that it has no part of what is "true." It is about taking what is already there and giving it a new form.

Literature can be a stay, or a foothold against despair. Is that enough? Of course it's not enough, but it's all we've got.

EMBRACE THE CRITICS

The one duty we owe to history is to rewrite it.

—OSCAR WILDE

EMBRACE THE CRITICS, ESPECIALLY the idiot who wounds you the deepest. Don't stew. Don't lash out. Don't talk behind his back. Walk up to him at the bar or coffee shop. Ask him if you can buy him a drink. Watch him sip. Sip your own. Thank him for his review. Clock his surprise. Pause a moment, then tell him—with a straight face— that it was the worst-written review you have read in a long time. Say it without anger. Don't walk away. Hold your stare. See if he has a sense of humor. If he understands you, and hangs around, and laughs, he just might be the critic you want. Go read his review again: he possibly has something important to tell you.

Every now and then there is nothing better than having somebody turn your work inside out. Still, the fundamental rule is, don't believe the critics, good or bad, but especially the good ones. The thing is that if you believe the good stuff, you must, by natural corollary, believe the bad.

Try not to become a reviewer yourself. Some writers do it bravely, but you're bound to hurt somebody along the way. Leave the reviewing to the reviewers.

In the end it's good advice to say, "Don't take any shit if you can possibly help it," because the fact of the matter is that the greatest load of shit will probably come from yourself. So, be humble. Be open to being your own critic. Every now and then we have to walk up to ourselves and buy that ugly mug of ours a drink.

BE EXHAUSTED WHEN YOU FINISH

> *When a reader falls in love with a book, it leaves its essence inside him, like radioactive fallout in an arable field, and after that there are certain crops that will no longer grow in him, while other, stranger, more fantastic growths may occasionally be produced.*
>
> —SALMAN RUSHDIE

YOU SHOULD BE EXHAUSTED WHEN YOU finish your story. You should feel as if you have just ripped yourself open and that there is nothing more to give. You should doubt yourself. You should be convinced that you are a charlatan. You should know that anything good you wrote was entirely accidental. You should be sure that you will never be able to do it again. You should have no idea how you got here and no idea if you will ever do it again. In fact, you should be convinced that you won't.

This exhaustion is the moment of greatest celebration: that's when you know you're almost finished.

YOUR LAST LINE

*If we are not sometimes baffled and amazed
and undone by the world around us, rendered
speechless and stunned, perhaps we are not
paying close enough attention.*

—BEN MARCUS

GOGOL SAID THAT THE LAST LINE OF
every story was, "And nothing would ever be the
same again." Nothing in life ever really begins in
one single place, and nothing ever truly ends. But
stories have at least to pretend to finish.

Don't tie it up too neatly. Don't try too much.
Often the story can end several paragraphs before,
so find the place to use your red pencil. Print out

several versions of the last sentence and sit with them. Go to your park bench again. Discover silence. Read each version over and over. Go with the one that you feel to be true and a little bit mysterious. Don't tack on the story's meaning. Don't moralize at the end. Don't preach that final hallelujah. Have faith that your reader has already gone with you on a long journey. They know where they have been. They know what they have learned. They know already that life is dark. You don't have to flood it with last-minute light.

You want the reader to remember. You want her to be changed. Or better still, to want to change.

Try, if possible, to finish in the concrete, with an action, a movement, to carry the reader forward. Never forget that a story begins long before you start it and ends long after you end it. Allow your reader to walk out from your last line and into her own imagination. Find some last-line grace. This is the true gift of writing. It is not yours anymore. It belongs in the elsewhere. It is the place you have created. Shake up their perception of the world. Combine worlds. Combine words.

Your last line is the first line for everybody else.

LETTER TO A YOUNG WRITER, REDUX

*That is the mystery about writing: it comes
out of afflictions, out of the gouged times,
when the heart is cut open.*

—EDNA O'BRIEN

YOUNG WRITER, HAS THE PASSION OF
our calling been robbed from us? It often seems
that the crisis of our age is that we are living in
stunned submission to the circumstances of the
times, the rule of politicians and bureaucrats and
hedge fund managers and others in their closed-
neck shirts. We are being bought off by our affair
with the contemporary drug of choice: ease. At the
same time, twisted social outrages are unfolding at
our feet. Political parties talk about building walls.

Universities invest in fossil fuels. Corporations celebrate themselves while pyres burn. The problem with so much of our reality is that it operates from a flat surface, a screen, and it does not address itself to the contoured world we live in. So, get off the couch. Get out the door. Onto the page. All of this is useless if it's just a pep talk. Your words are not a consolation prize. Justify your rage. Take pleasure in the recklessness of your own imagination. So much writing nowadays seems to suffer from a reduced moral authority, not just in the minds of the readers, but in the minds and indeed the language of the writers ourselves. Writing is no longer part of our national idea. We don't look to our authors in the way we did decades ago. Nobody fears what we have to say. Why is that? We have allowed our voices to be devalued in favor of comfort. Our moral compass is off-kilter. We have given in to the tendency to be neutralized. We live in a culture where increasingly we are mapped—we have GPS'd ourselves to death. We have forgotten how to get properly lost. This is not some bleeding-heart simplicity, nor should your response to it be. So, embrace the challenge. Never forget that writing is the freedom to articulate yourself against power. It is a form of nonviolent engagement and civil disobedience. You have to stand outside society, beyond coercion, intimidation, cruelty, duress. Where power wants to simplify, you should complicate. Where power wants to moralize, you should criticize. Where power wants to intimidate, embrace. The amazing thing about good writing is that it can find the pulse of the wound without having to inflict the actual violence. It is a way of recognizing the hurt without praising it or suffering it. Writing allows the illusion of pain, while forcing us to grow up and recognize our own demons. We touch the electricity of suffering, but we can, eventually, recover. We carry the scars, but that's all they are: scars. We have to understand that language is power, no matter how often power tries to strip us of language. Want to know your enemy? Read their books. Watch their plays. Examine their poetry. Try to get to the heart of them. The grievance you know is so much better than the unknown. The impulse to change comes from encountering the multiple and complex shades of the world. Be aware of what you are writing against. Stand up. Be aware that to be a hero, you might have to be able to be the fool. Alas, poor Yorick, poor Citizen, poor Falstaff, the role of the hero often seems ridiculous, but the best of them are willing to play it anyway. Against war. Against greed. Against walls. Against simplicity. Against shallow ignorance. The fool should speak the truth, even when—or maybe especially when—it's unpopular. Don't be embarrassed. Don't give up. Don't be cowed into silence. Stand on the outside. Become more dangerous. Have people fear your bite. Restore that which has been devalued by others. Don't let the passion of your calling be ridiculed. Raise your voice on behalf of those who have been drowned out. Don't allow the begrudgers to render you useless. Value the cynic. Yes, praise him even. He is useful. He is one you can still teach. Don't back away from engagement. You must talk about the grime and the poverty and the injustice and the thousand other everyday torments. You must speak of life no matter how bitter or lacerating. Our writing is a living portrait of ourselves. Good sentences have the ability to shock, seduce, and drag us out of our stupor. Be what a diamond is to glass. Scrape your way across. Transform what has been seen. Imagine the immensities of experience. Oppose the cruelties. Break the silence. Be prepared to risk yourself. Find radiance. Ready yourself for scorn. Embrace difficulty. Work hard. Face it, you're not going to write a masterpiece before breakfast. Your song will exact a price. Be prepared to pay. Write, young writer, write. Claim your proper future. Find the language. Write for the sheer pleasure we take in doing it, but also for the knowledge that it might just shift this world of ours a little. It is, after all, a beautiful and strange and furious place. Literature reminds us that life is not already written down. There are still infinite possibilities. Make from your confrontation with despair a tiny little margin of beauty. The more you choose to see, the more you will see. In the end, the only things worth doing are the things that might possibly break your heart. Rage on.

Yours very truly,

Colum McCann

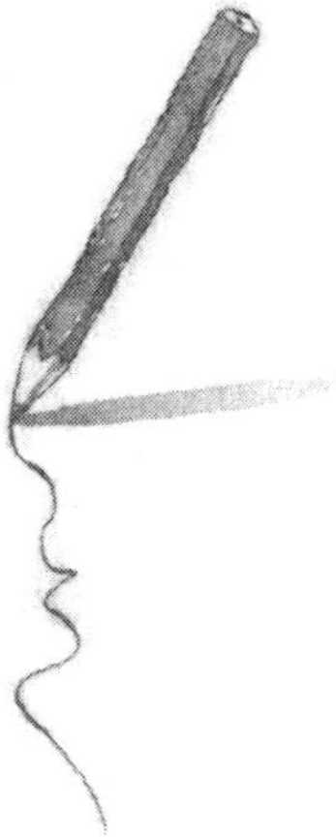

Colum McCann is the internationally
bestselling author of the novels *TransAtlantic,*
Let the Great World Spin, Zoli, Dancer, This
Side of Brightness, and *Songdogs,* as well as
three critically acclaimed story collections.
His fiction has been published in forty
languages. He has received many honors,
including the National Book Award, the
International IMPAC Dublin Literary Award,
a Chevalier des Arts et des Lettres award
from the French government, and the Ireland
Fund of Monaco Literary Award in Memory
of Princess Grace. He has been named one of
Esquire's "Best and Brightest," and his short
film *Everything in This Country Must* was
nominated for an Oscar in 2005. In 2017 he

was inducted into the American Academy of Arts and Letters. A contributor to *The New Yorker, The New York Times Magazine, The Atlantic,* and *The Paris Review,* he teaches in the Hunter College MFA Creative Writing program. He lives in New York City with his wife and their three children, and he is the cofounder of the global nonprofit story exchange organization, Narrative 4.

colummccann.com
Facebook.com/colummccannauthor

To inquire about booking Colum McCann for a speaking engagement, please contact the Penguin Random House Speakers Bureau at speakers@penguinrandomhouse.com.

A B O U T   T H E   T Y P E

This book was set in Caslon, a typeface first designed in 1722 by William Caslon (1692–1766). Its widespread use by most English printers in the early eighteenth century soon supplanted the Dutch typefaces that had formerly prevailed. The roman is considered a "workhorse" typeface due to its pleasant, open appearance, while the italic is exceedingly decorative.

Don't let the

blank page

shrink-wrap your

mind